Reimagining the Body of Christ in Paul's Letters

Reimagining the Body of Christ in Paul's Letters

IN VIEW OF PAUL'S GOSPEL

Yung Suk Kim

RESOURCE *Publications* • Eugene, Oregon

REIMAGINING THE BODY OF CHRIST IN PAUL'S LETTERS
In View of Paul's Gospel

Copyright © 2019 Yung Suk Kim. All rights reserved. Except for brief quotations in critical publications or reviews, no part of this book may be reproduced in any manner without prior written permission from the publisher. Write: Permissions, Wipf and Stock Publishers, 199 W. 8th Ave., Suite 3, Eugene, OR 97401.

Resource Publications
An Imprint of Wipf and Stock Publishers
199 W. 8th Ave., Suite 3
Eugene, OR 97401

www.wipfandstock.com

PAPERBACK ISBN: 978-1-5326-7776-2
HARDCOVER ISBN: 978-1-5326-7777-9
EBOOK ISBN: 978-1-5326-7778-6

Manufactured in the U.S.A.   APRIL 23, 2019

Contents

Preface vii

1. Introduction 1
   The Body of Christ and Paul's Gospel 1
   The Diverse Use of the Body of Christ 3

2. Christ Crucified 7
   The Cause of Jesus's Crucifixion 7
   Early Christian Interpretation of Jesus's Crucifixion 10
   Christ Crucified and the Gospel 18

3. The Body of Christ at the Lord's Supper 21
   The Kernel Story of the Lord's Supper 22
   Retelling the Lord's Supper 26
   Ethical Exhortations 28

4. The Body of Christ and the Community 30
   Rigid Unity or Soft Union 31
   The Body of Christ as a Metaphor for Living 35

5. Reclaiming Christ's Body for the Embodiment of God's Gospel 40
   The Body in Context: The Greco-Roman World and Paul 41
   Who is Paul? What Caused Him to Change? 43
   The Body Metaphor in Paul's Letters 45

Contents

Christ's Body as a Metaphor of Holism 47
Christ's Body as His Sacrifice and Embodiment of God's Righteousness 49
Christ's Body as an Ethic of Christian Life 50
Recovering the Lost Tradition: Dynamic Aspects of Faith 52

Bibliography 55

Preface

THOSE WHO HAVE POWER prefer unity to diversity. They do not want a diversity of thoughts. They are afraid of losing everything if their rule or leadership is challenged. But everyday people are not really concerned about unity. Rather, they need more respect, dignity, and equality in their lives. Often unity becomes the language of control. This is true to the case of the Roman Empire. Even if diversity is allowed in the Empire, it is limited to religion and culture. That is, people are prohibited from protesting against the rule of Rome. They must speak the language of Rome. They are told again and again that society is one body with an emphasis on unity. In the name of unity, the suffering of the unfortunate is taken for granted.

Even in the church, pastors talk about the unity of the church, based on 1 Cor 12:27 ("You are the body of Christ and individually parts of it"). In their preaching, members of the church are expected to think in the same way without asking questions about the church doctrine or any teachings about God. In a traditional frame of interpretation, scholars read "the body of Christ" as a social body with an emphasis on unity (*homonoia*) just like Stoics who tell members of the society to be one without asking about injustices.

But Paul does not mean that members of the community have to be in consensus in all matters; rather, his emphasis is they have to have the same mind of Christ. In other words, they must live like Christ, being ruled by his spirit, imitating his faith. An

PREFACE

alternative reading of this body metaphor is "a way of living." So the point is: "You are the Christic body. You are to be ruled by Christ, individually and communally." This way of reading of the Greek genitive is certainly plausible as we see in Rom 6:6: "The body of sin might be destroyed." Here, "the body of sin" is construed as the "sinful body" or the "sin-ruled body."

In this alternative reading of the body metaphor in 1 Cor 12:12-27, Paul's emphasis is not merely the lack of unity in the community but the lack of a true diversity due to the lack of Christic embodiment. Some Corinthians claim that they are wise in Christ and were saved already. Others boast about their gift of the spirit: speaking in tongues, prophesying, and even their knowledge. Given the problem of the disembodiment of Christ, Paul asks them to identify with Christ and follow his spirit. For example, in 1 Cor 6:12-20, the Corinthians are advised not to sleep with prostitutes because they are parts (*mele*) of Christ. Here, we have an image of Christ's body as a human body, not as a social body. Because they are connected to Christ, they must behave accordingly. Then they can glorify God in their body (1 Cor 6:20).

This book questions all familiar readings of "the body of Christ" and helps readers rethink the context and the purpose of this body metaphor in view of Paul's gospel. Against the view that Paul's body of Christ metaphor mainly has to do with a metaphorical organism that emphasizes unity, I argue that the body of Christ metaphor has more to do with the embodiment of God's gospel through Christ. While Deutero-Pauline Letters and Pastoral Letters use the body of Christ mainly as an organism, Paul's Undisputed Letters, in particular, 1 Corinthians and Romans, treat it differently with a focus on Christic embodiment. We will reevaluate the diverse use of "the body of Christ" in Paul's undisputed letters: Christ crucified (the crucified body of Christ); "the body of Christ" at the Lord's Supper; and "the body of Christ" and the community. In all of these, the body of Christ" in Paul's undisputed letters has to do with the proclamation of the gospel.

1

Introduction

The Body of Christ and Paul's Gospel

THERE ARE DIVERSE CONCEPTS of "the body of Christ" in Paul's undisputed letters. This book examines the body of Christ only in Paul's undisputed letters because those letters reflect his theology. Otherwise, Deutero-Pauline and Pastoral Letters have a very different use of the body of Christ that hardly comes from Paul's own theology. While we often contrast the starking differences between them, our focus is to stay in his authentic letters and to examine his view of the body of Christ. In these undisputed letters, he talks about Christ crucified (the crucified body of Christ), "the body of Christ" at the Lord's Supper, and "the body of Christ" and the community. Each of these concepts needs reexamination in view of his gospel.

Overall, "the body of Christ" in Paul's undisputed letters has to do with his proclamation of the gospel characterized with threefold dimensions: God's righteousness, Christ's faithfulness, and Christian participation in Christ.[1] Paul's gospel begins with God, who is righteous and cares for the poor, orphans, and widows. He

---

1. Yung Suk Kim, *A Theological Introduction to Paul's Letters: Exploring a Threefold Theology of Paul* (Eugene, OR: Cascade, 2011), 1–37.

states that he was "set apart for the gospel of God" (Rom 1:1), which is none other than "the power of God for salvation for everyone who has faith" (Rom 1:16). But this good news of God needs Jesus, declared to be the Son of God, who demonstrated God's righteousness (Rom 1:4; 3:22). Jesus's work of God was possible through his faithfulness.[2] He was crucified because he was weak, but God raised him from the dead. His sacrifice was commemorated at the Lord's Supper. Whenever and wherever Christians (those who follow Jesus and participate in his faithfulness) meet, they have to follow his spirit. Individually and communally, they are the body of Christ (1 Cor 12:27).

Traditionally, "the body of Christ" in 1 Cor 12:27 has been understood as a metaphorical organism that emphasizes the unity of the community. But alternatively, it can be read as a metaphor for a way of living, in the sense of an attributive genitive: "the Christic body." A similar use of this genitive is found in Rom 6:6: "the body of sin" as "the sinful body."[3] Accordingly, we can translate 1 Cor 12:27 as follows: "You are the Christic body and parts constituting Christ." Here the implication is not merely that "you are one because you belong to a body or a community" ("the traditional view of a metaphorical organism") but that "you are united to Christ and therefore you have to embody Christ." This idea is also found in 1 Cor 6:17: "But anyone united to the Lord becomes one spirit with him").

---

2. Πίστεως Χριστοῦ (*pistis christou* in Rom 3:22 and Gal 2:16) can be better understood as the subjective genitive case. "Faith in Christ" does not seem to reflect Paul' view because, for example, in Rom 3:22, he distinguishes between *pistis christou* and "all who have faith." The former must be Christ's faith whereas the latter is faith of those who follow Jesus. His point is that Jesus, the Son of God, manifested God's righteousness through faith. Because of this faithful work of Jesus, all those who follow him also must live righteously before God.

3. Yung Suk Kim, *Christ's Body in Corinth: The Politics of a Metaphor* (Minneapolis, MN: Fortress, 2008), 11–96. See also Yung Suk Kim, "Reclaiming Christ's Body: Embodiment of God's Gospel in Paul's Letters," *Interpretation* 67.1 (2013): 20–29.

INTRODUCTION

The Diverse Use of the Body of Christ

In the following, we will see briefly the diverse use of the body of Christ in Paul's undisputed letters. First, Paul often uses the image of Christ crucified when he emphasizes "the gospel of Christ."[4] For example, in 1 Cor 2:2, he says: "For I decided to know nothing among you except Jesus Christ, and him crucified." The crucified body of Christ is also a type of the body, which was broken and maimed for "the gospel of God."[5] Therefore, Christians (those who follow Jesus and share his faithfulness) also "have died to the law through the body of Christ" (Rom 7:4). Here "the body of Christ" evokes the image of his crucifixion.[6]

Second, Paul also uses the other concept of the body of Christ at the Lord's Supper, as in 1 Cor 11:17–34. It is a Eucharistic body of Christ. Paul delivers the word of the Lord's Supper: "This is my body that is for you. Do this in remembrance of me" (1 Cor 11:24). Jesus's death is commemorated, and his faith must be followed by those who follow him. At the Lord's Supper, they celebrate Jesus Christ's life and his death by sharing the bread and wine.

---

4. "The gospel of Christ" appears in Paul's letters: Gal 1:7; 1 Cor 9:12; 2 Cor 9:13; Phil 1:27; 3:2. The gospel of Christ can be understood as his work of God.

5. "The gospel of God" appears in Rom 1:1, 9; 15:16; 1 Thess 2:2, 8–9. Jesus's work of God can be understood as proclaiming "the gospel of God." His crucifixion is resulted from his challenging message and work of God.

6. Paul does not reject the law *per se*, as he clearly says in Rom 3:31: "Do we then overthrow the law by this faith? By no means! On the contrary, we uphold the law." Paul's point is not that the law is evil or useless but that it cannot overwrite "the law of God" (Rom 7:22, 25)—understood as God's love and justice that are extended to all, Jews and Gentiles. Then God's law can be followed by "the law of faith" (Rom 3:27). This law of faith is confirmed by Jesus when he lived for God, risking his life and giving it up. Ultimately, Paul's point is that faith is required from beginning to end, as he says in Rom 3:30: "since God is one; and he will justify the circumcised on the ground of faith and the uncircumcised through that same faith." His logic of explaining the primacy of faith over the law is found in Romans 4:13–25 where God's promise precedes anything such as the law or even faith. God's grace or promise comes first. Then faith comes. God calls Abraham and makes a covenant with him. Abraham trusts God and follows him. That is his faith. The law was given later through Moses and its purpose is not to convict people but to guide them.

Third, Paul also extensively talks about the body of Christ as a metaphor and relates it to the community. In 1 Cor 12:12–27, he uses the human body as an analogy and connects to the body of Christ. In Rom 12:4–5, he also talks about the body of Christ and its relationship to the community. Traditionally, the body of Christ has been understood as a metaphorical organism. That is, "the body of Christ" is Christ's church or community. This use of the body is popular in Stoicism during Paul's time. The society is one body with bonded hierarchy. This metaphorical use of the body is also very clear in Deutero-Pauline Letters (Col 1:18, 24; Eph 4:12; 5:23). But in Paul's undisputed letters, "the body of Christ" may be interpreted differently. In 1 Cor 12:12–27, Paul talks about the human body and its relationship with Christ and the community. 1 Cor 12:12 reads: "For just as the body is one and has many members, and all the members of the body, though many, are one body, so it is with Christ." The primary source or image of the body comes from the human body. Stoicism's view of the human body is hierarchical and emphasizes unity. But Paul thinks differently and sees it as a holistic entity that different parts work together in a body to benefit other parts. Namely, all parts are essential and respectful and edify the body. Parts relationship is complementary, and it is not seen through the mode of competition or hierarchical unity that justifies sacrifice. This idea of the human body is well articulated in 1 Cor 12:13–26. When one part rejoices, all rejoice together. Conversely, when one part suffers, all other parts also suffer together. All parts are united to a body and share a common destiny in a good way. Weaker parts are treated well with due respect. As seen here, Paul's view of the human body is different from Stoicism's in that weaker parts have to serve the strong parts. Stoicism emphasizes the oneness and unity of society in order to maintain the status quo.

For Paul, the body is one not because it is a unified system that maintains or promotes the sameness, concord, or unity at the expense of differences or diversity, but because it is a united whole to which all parts work together in solidarity with each other. Here the purpose of union with a body is not to reach concord

INTRODUCTION

or unity but to live a life full of love and justice. For example, in 1 Cor 6:12–20, Paul talks about the Corinthians' unethical lifestyle and their sexual immorality by way of "the body of Christ" and a prostitute. He asks: "Do you not know that your bodies are parts (μέλη, *mele*) of Christ? Should I therefore take the parts of Christ and make them parts of a prostitute? Never! Do you not know that whoever is united to a prostitute becomes one body with her? For it is said, 'The two shall be one flesh'" (1 Cor 6:15–16). Here, μέλη (*mele*) is the plural of μέλος (*melos*), which means a part of the body. Even though *mele* can be interpreted as members of the church, body parts of the Christ make a better sense because Paul talks about members' union with Christ through the image of the human body. Since they are united to Christ, they must behave accordingly "in a manner worthy of the gospel of Christ" (Phil 1:27).

Likewise, we can understand differently the familiar phrase "the body of Christ" in 1 Cor 12:12–27. In 1 Cor 12:12, the human body analogy is associated with Christ: "For just as the body is one and has many members, and all the members of the body, though many, are one body, so it is with Christ." In other words, the way the human body is seen, as seen above, also applies to Christ. Christ is a person, who is understood in connection with the human body. Paul's point is that Christ is a body—not in the sense of organism—to which Christians are united. That is, Christians, though they are different in terms of abilities or functions, are to work together in good and bad times because they are connected with Christ. They are one not merely because they constitute a Christian community, just as Stoics say similarly that the society is one, but because they have fellowship with Christ, sharing his spirit. What matters is not mere membership or belongingness to a church but how to maintain fellowship with Christ. Therefore, Paul's conclusion is in 1 Cor 12:27: "You (plural) are Christ's body and individually members of it." This verse can be understood in light of ethical union with Christ. That is, the Corinthians have to embody Christ, and that is what it means to constitute the body of Christ. A possible translation will be: "You are the Christic body and individually constitute the body."

We may also understand Rom 12:4–5 similarly: "For as in one body we have many members, and not all the members have the same function, so we, who are many, are one body in Christ, and individually we are members one of another." Paul emphasizes the importance of mutual care in the community because they (Romans) are one body in Christ. Here "one body" can be understood, as we saw in the case of 1 Cor 12:12–27, through the mutually beneficial body mechanism. This kind of human body should apply to the Christian community. So he says that it is "one body in Christ," which echoes "so it is with Christ" in 1 Cor 12:12. In Rom 12:5, just like 1 Cor 12:27b, Paul says similar things about the embodiment of Christ in a Christian community. That is, Roman Christians are members of the body, which is Christ. So they have to help each other and edify the community because they are parts (μέλη, *mele*) of Christ (like the human body). "Individually members of one another" means they are not separate from each other, and more importantly, they belong to Christ, and they have to live like Christ. In other words, Paul's point is not simply that they belong to Christ or that they are one but that they have to follow the Spirit of Christ. This idea is found in Rom 8:9–10: "Anyone who does not have the Spirit of Christ does not belong to him. But if Christ is in you, though the body is dead because of sin, the Spirit is life because of righteousness."

# 2

Christ Crucified

CHRIST CRUCIFIED LIES AT the center of Paul's gospel proclamation, as he says in 1 Cor 2:2: "For I decided to know nothing among you except Jesus Christ, and him crucified." In this chapter, first of all, we will fully explore what it means to be put to death by crucifixion in the first-century Roman world. That is, we need to know what is the cause of Jesus's crucifixion. Then, we will see how Christians interpreted Jesus's death differently. That is, we need to know the implications of the cross as they lived with the gospel. Then, we will see how Paul relates the message of Christ crucified to his gospel.

The Cause of Jesus's Crucifixion

Crucifixion is reserved for slaves and criminals who commit a political crime against the Empire. If they rebel against Rome, they would face a most painful form of death with a public display. Likewise, enemies of the state are cruelly smacked down and crucified. Josephus writes that Alexander Janneus (103–76 BCE) crucified eight hundred Pharisees while their children and wives were watching the scene. He also writes about the crucifixion during Titus's siege of Jerusalem and calls it "the most wretched deaths." Philo also tells that at the time of Caligula (37–41 CE), many Jews were tortured and crucified in the amphitheater of Alexandria. In all of this, the message is clear in that anyone who challenges Rome will face the horrible death of crucifixion, which is a most shameful, painful, slow-dying form of death. Jesus was also crucified by Rome because he was considered dangerous to Rome. In fact, he was called the King of Jews according to the Gospels. He was tortured and publicly humiliated by Rome's power. His body was broken, maimed, and remained on the cross for a few days. Again, the message is clear in that anyone who challenges Rome will face such an excruciating death. Rome is only the great power, and all others are less and inferior. Rome declares that Jesus is nothing and that Rome is the only kingdom where the emperor is the only king and power. In this situation, Jesus is declared to be the Son of God (Rom 1:4). But there is only one Son of God in the Roman Empire. Jesus's teaching of the kingdom of God is radical and unacceptable to the Roman authority because he embraces the lowly and the poor. He breaks down the norm of a society built on knowledge and power as well as the social boundary between the strong and the weak. He sits with the sinner and prostitutes and eats with them. He even breaks Jewish laws to keep them holy. He heals the sick on the sabbath, which is forbidden according to the Pharisaic interpretation of the sabbatical law. He challenges Jerusalem and its leadership too. He even disrupts the temple economy by overturning money change tables and expelling business people from the temple. To both sides of Rome and Jerusalem, he is a potential danger. Therefore, it is very plausible, as the gospel stories imply, that Jewish leaders and Roman authority had the same interest in removing Jesus from his place. If his teaching about God had not been challenging Rome, he would not have been captured and crucified. Ultimately, crucifixion is the Roman event and it is impossible without Rome's approval.

Therefore, we should not be confused about his death. He was not destined to die for humanity or the world. His death is the result of what he said and did for God's kingdom or rule against Rome's rule. In spite of his death, Jesus was not defeated because God raised him from the dead and made him be the Lord of all. The above argument that Jesus's "dangerous" teaching and action against Rome led him to death is supported by the gospel accounts. All four gospels basically confirm that Jesus's death is the result of his proclamation about God, who must rule the world with justice. Though the details of his words and deeds in each gospel are different, the main reason for his death/crucifixion remains the same. For example, in the synoptic gospels, he advocates for the marginalized and social outcasts through his teaching and healing. Because of this, he is gradually opposed by leaders and other people, arrested by Roman soldiers, tried before Pilate, and crucified by them. Even in John's Gospel, Jesus's death is gradual and he is crucified due to his work of God.

Paul also has a similar view of Jesus who revealed God's righteousness through faith. Paul's *pistis christou* in Rom 3:22 should be understood as Christ's faith, not "faith in Christ." That is, Paul states that God's righteousness has been manifested through Christ's faith. God's righteousness is close to God's kingdom or rule in the synoptic gospels. God's righteousness means that God is the righteous one who must rule the world with justice. Christ's faith means his trust in God and his commitment to the gospel of God. In Rom 1:4, Paul says that Jesus was declared to be the Son of God with power. This sonship is because of his faith in God and his work of God. Paul's thinking is that God's righteousness will not be available without faith. Jesus is the Messiah and Son of God who radically manifested who God is through faith. Jesus did not spare his life in doing so.

As we see above, Jesus is led to the crucifixion because of his work of God, because of Roman authority's torture, and because of Jewish leaders' collusion with Rome. But Paul articulates the cause of Jesus's death in still another way, as in 2 Cor 13:4: "For he was crucified by weakness (ἐξ ἀσθενείας, *eks astheneias*), but lives by the power of God (ἐκ δυνάμεως θεοῦ, *ek dunameos theou*). For we are weak in him, but in dealing with you we will live with him by the power of God." Paul plainly acknowledges that Jesus was weak and therefore he was crucified. He was not a God or an angel who cannot die. He had a body susceptible to violence and death. He was a real human being. The only way he could avoid the crucifixion was to stop his work on the kingdom of God. *Ex astheneias* (ἐξ ἀσθενείας) is often translated as "in weakness," as in the NRSV. But I am suspicious that this translation echoes the idea of Jesus's voluntary, redemptive suffering. If he had meant "in weakness," he would have used *en astheneias*, which means straight "in weakness." Therefore, "in weakness" is not a good translation because it does not convey the idea of weakness as the cause of his crucifixion. While the Greek preposition *ek* means several things such as separation ("from, out of, or away from"), "the direction from which something comes," and origin, cause or reason ("as a result of, or because of"), it is not close to the preposition "in." In this verse, the preposition *ek* has more to do with "cause or reason" because there is a contrast between *eks astheneias* and *ek dunameos theou*. Namely, Jesus was crucified by weakness (in the sense that "because of weakness"), but lives by the power of God (*ek dunameos theou*). Here weakness (*astheneias*) refers to Jesus's humanity. The only way he could avoid his crucifixion was to stop proclaiming the good news of God or challenging Rome and Jerusalem. Otherwise, if he was willing to testify to the good news of God, he could not avoid his cross. It is through Jesus Christ's faith that God's righteousness was revealed in the world (Rom 3:21–26).

Early Christian Interpretation of Jesus's Crucifixion

Jesus's crucifixion is sad, difficult news for his followers to accept. In Jewish tradition, someone dying on the cross is a curse by God (Deut 21:22–23). From the eyes of Jews, Jesus did not liberate them from the rule of Rome. Rather, he was weak and foolish. But early Christians claimed that he has risen. While some of them believe that their salvation is done once and for all because of Jesus's one-time heroic, redemptive death, others do not believe that, arguing there are remaining works to do after Jesus is gone. So much so, as the Christian history shows, this debate about the meaning of the cross has not come to an end. Even within the New Testament, there are different understandings of the cross. Therefore, what we need is not to take one view among others but to discern multiple implications of Jesus's death. Even when we talk about Paul's language of Jesus's cross, there are multiple dimensions of the cross event because it involves religion, politics, ethics, and personal life. One single event of the cross does not mean it has a single meaning or implication. In the following, therefore, we will see what Paul brings to readers in terms of the meaning of the cross.

God's Love on the Cross

God's love is seen on the cross, as Paul says: "But God proves his love for us in that while we still were sinners Christ died for us" (Rom 5:8). Paul argues that the Christ event shows God's love. That is, through Christ's faith that he did not spare his life to reveal God, people realize how God's love is great, receive the grace of God, and know how they should live.[1] So Paul says: God "did not withdraw his own Son, but gave him up for all of us" (Rom 8:32). This statement of 8:32 must be confessional in that everything is under God's providence. Otherwise, it should not be taken literally in the sense that Jesus's crucifixion is planned by God. Rather, God takes Jesus's faith and his sacrifice as a moment of changing human history. Rom 3:24–26 shows this point:

> They are now justified by his grace as a gift, through the redemption that is in Christ Jesus, whom God put forward as *hilasterion* by his blood, effective through faith. He did this to show his righteousness, because in his divine forbearance he had passed over the sins previously committed; it was to prove at the present time that he himself is righteous and that he justifies the one who has *faith of Jesus* (πίστεως Ἰησοῦ).

In Rom 3:24, Paul says one's justification is made by God's grace as a gift. This means that God is love and the source of

---

1. Arnfridur Gudmundsdottir, *Meeting God on the Cross: Christ, the Cross, and the Feminist Critique* (New York: Oxford University Press, 2011), 155. See also Yung Suk Kim, *Resurrecting Jesus: The Renewal of New Testament Theology* (Eugene, OR: Cascade, 2015), 74–90.

justification. God is the one who justifies those who live faithfully. But humans failed to live by faith, as Paul shows this case in Rom 1–2; rather, they were crooked and disloyal to God. So from God's perspective, there must be a radical example of faith. That is Jesus Christ who was obedient to God until he died. The redemption is made in Christ Jesus, whom God considers as *hilasterion* (ἱλαστήριον), which is a mercy seat (*kapporet* on the Day of Atonement, Exod 25:17). The action to render on Jesus's death is God, but the one who was put to death or was willing to die is Jesus. God recognizes Jesus's faith and his sacrifice. Thus, God is moved by his Son, and his Spirit is there with him. God is present with Jesus on the cross, which is none other than the "mercy seat." Through Christ's sacrifice and his faith, one may enter into a good relationship with God. Furthermore, God passed over "the sins previously committed" (Rom 3:25) because of Jesus's act of faith. Now is a new time that people may be hopeful again because of Jesus's example of faith. They may live by faith because of him. Thus, in Rom 3:26, Paul concludes as follows: "It was to prove at the present time that he himself is righteous and that he justifies the one who has the faithfulness of Jesus." God proves his righteousness through his Son Jesus because of his faith. God also justifies the one who has Jesus's faith.

In sum, when we say God's love is seen on the cross, it does not mean that God planned his Son's death for a sin-offering to deal with sins. Rather, it means that Jesus demonstrated God's love at the risk of his life and that God considered Jesus's death and his faith as a locus of reconciliation with God.[2] That is, God recognizes Jesus's faith and sacrifice and decides to open a new time of salvation.

Jesus's Love on the Cross

Jesus's love is seen on the cross, as 2 Cor 5:14–15 indicates: "For the love of Christ urges us on, because we are convinced that one

2. Yung Suk Kim, "Hilasterion in Rom 3:25: Jesus as a New Locus of Reconciliation," article in progress.

has died for all; therefore all have died. And he died for all, so that those who live might live no longer for themselves, but for him who died and was raised for them." Here "Jesus's death for all" can be understood as his unwavering faith that God is righteous and steadfast. He did not spare his life because of his commitment to the love and justice of God. He advocated God's love for the sinners and the oppressed. Paul affirms Jesus's love about Roman Christians: "Who is to condemn? It is Christ Jesus, who died, yes, who was raised, who is at the right hand of God, who indeed intercedes for us. Who will separate us from the love of Christ? Will hardship, or distress, or persecution, or famine, or nakedness, or peril, or sword?" (Rom 8:34–35). In the end, Paul says, the love of Christ is compared to the love of God because God's love is manifested through Christ: "For I am convinced that neither death, nor life, nor angels, nor rulers, nor things present, nor things to come, nor powers, nor height, nor depth, nor anything else in all creation, will be able to separate us from the love of God in Christ Jesus our Lord" (Rom 8:38–39).

The love of Christ also can be understood as his love of people and the world.[3] "One has died for all" means Jesus's sacrifice for all humanity. At this time, Paul uses the active voice in that Jesus died for all, which is his decision and action out of his love. Even though he was put to death by the Roman authority, there is another dimension of his death which we must point out: that is his love of the world and humanity. Scholars interpret differently Jesus's love on the cross. Traditionally, Jesus's love on the cross has been understood as his vicarious, redemptive death for all. But perhaps this view is not seen in Paul. There are attempts to reinterpret the meaning of Jesus's love on the cross. Anna Mercedes argues that Jesus's love must be understood as his self-giving love (*kenosis*), which is voluntary and should not read as a loss of the self.[4] But this view is a very romanticized one in that there is no

---

3. See Yung Suk Kim, *Messiah in Weakness: A Portrait of Jesus from the Perspective of the Dispossessed* (Eugene, OR: Cascade, 2016), 106–118.

4. Anna Mercedes, *Power For: Feminism and Christ's Self-giving* (London: T&T Clark, 2011).

talk of a tragic death of the crucifixion. The question is: How can we talk about his self-giving love without talking out his loss of the self? The other approach I find interesting is Wendy Farley's feminist reading of the cross event. Carefully distinguishing between suffering which is evil and Jesus's love for humanity, she observes: "Suffering tells us we are unredeemable. The passion tells us that we are saved and always were and always will be."[5] She strikes a balance between bad suffering and good salvation because of Jesus's cross. But what lacks in her reading is that there is no looking at Jesus's work of God. The other interesting approach comes from M. Shawn Copeland, who reads Jesus's cross through the experience of African-American lynching and deaths. So much so that she points out the tragic, evil death of Jesus and sees Jesus as the one who has solidarity with the oppressed.[6] This reading is fair enough to point out the ugly face of Roman torture done to Jesus and also to see Jesus's solidarity with the marginalized from the cross. As a Pauline scholar, I can push further to include Jesus's work of God, which led him to death. That is, he could not stop working to advocate for the poor and marginalized.[7] In other words, Jesus's cross is not the only moment when he has solidarity with them. In this light, "one's dying for all" (2 Cor 5:14) does not necessarily mean a vicarious death as in the traditional atonement theories. If we understand "Jesus's death for all" as his voluntary selfless love for humanity and as the result of his work of God, the traditional atonement theories do not stand here. This book argues that Paul does not present the view of a sin-offering by Jesus's death. In the Deutero-Pauline letters and Hebrews (Eph 1:7; 2:13; 1 Pet 1:2, 19; Heb 2:17; 9:14), there is an idea that the blood of

---

5. Wendy Farley, *Gathering Those Driven Away: A Theology of Incarnation* (Louisville, KY: Westminster John Knox Press, 2011), 164.

6. M. Shawn Copeland, *Enfleshing Freedom: Body, Race, and Being* (Minneapolis, MN: Fortress, 2011), 99.

7. This is the view of liberation theology in that Jesus is seen as a freedom-justice fighter. For example, see Yung Suk Kim and Jin-ho Kim, eds. *Reading Minjung Theology in the Twenty-first Century: Selected Writings by Ahn Byung-mu and Modern, Critical Responses* (Eugene, OR: Pickwick, 2013).

Jesus purifies sinners. But in Paul's authentic letters, Jesus's death has more to do with Christ's love of God and the world.

Obviously, Paul's letters include the idea of atonement. For example, 1 Cor 15:3 reads: "For I handed on to you as of first importance what I in turn had received: that Christ died for our sins in accordance with the scriptures." However, the meaning of the "Christ died for our sins" is not clear because the preposition *hyper* (ὑπὲρ) is ambiguous. *Hyper* means "for, in behalf of, concerning." One possibility is that Jesus died "instead of us" to deal with sins. This view of atonement is found in traditional atonement theories such as penal substitution theory, ransom theory, and satisfaction theory. That is, Jesus's death is vicarious and redemptive, and his suffering is necessary. But this view hardly makes a sense to Paul because Jesus's death alone is not enough. He always asks his congregations to die with Christ. For example, Rom 6:8 says: "But if we have died with Christ, we believe that we will also live with him." Rom 7: 4 says: "you have died to the law through the body of Christ." 2 Cor 5:14 says: "For the love of Christ urges us on, because we are convinced that one has died for all; therefore all have died." Gal 2:19 says: "For through the law I died to the law, so that I might live to God. I have been crucified with Christ."

The other meaning of *hyper* is that Jesus died "because of our sins." In other words, Jesus died because "we did not live up to God's will." "Our sins" include all kinds of sins that reject the wisdom of God. So "dying for people" can be a moral sacrifice that he showed God's love and his justice at the risk of his life. Like Christ, people also have to die. 2 Cor 5:14–15 makes clear that because Christ died for all, they all have died. So they have to follow his footsteps so that God's love may be proven (Rom 5:8). They should live not for themselves but for God and others (2 Cor 5:15). Paul also says in Rom 6:3–4: "Do you not know that all of us who have been baptized into Christ Jesus were baptized into his death? Therefore we have been buried with him by baptism into death, so that, just as Christ was raised from the dead by the glory of the Father, we too might walk in newness of life" (c.f., 1 Thess 5:10).

Similarly, we can read Rom 5:8 in light of Jesus's love: "But God proves his love for us in that while we still were sinners Christ *died for us*" (see also 1 Thess 5:9–10). In this text, the preposition *hyper* is ambiguous: "for, in behalf of, concerning." As we saw before, the traditional atonement theory is not the only option to read. Paul emphasizes Christ's love of God and the world. Paul's logic is not that because Christ died, "you do not die," but that because Christ died, "you also have died with him" (c.f, 2 Cor 5:14; Gal 2:19).

God's Judgment on the Cross

God's judgment is also seen on the cross because Jesus's death is not only a tragic event but an unjust, evil one that cannot be condoned.[8] In 1 Cor 1, Paul deconstructs the wisdom of the world through Christ crucified and argues that "God's foolishness is wiser than human wisdom, and that God's weakness is stronger than human strength" (1 Cor 1:25). To find his argument further, we need to read closely 1 Cor 1:17–31. In this text, Paul reminds them that the cross of Jesus involves God's judgment on all who do not seek God's wisdom and his strength. Here, he responds to the Corinthians who boast about their wisdom and strength. God's foolishness means God is seen foolish when he cares for the foolish (all those who are uneducated and live on the edge of society). Likewise, Jesus's advocating for the foolish looks foolish. But what he did shows the power of God. Jesus did not spare his life to reveal God's righteousness. So the message about the cross involves God's power, as 1 Cor 1:17–18 says: "For Christ did not send me to baptize but to proclaim the gospel, and not with eloquent wisdom, so that the cross of Christ might not be emptied of its power. For the message about the cross is foolishness to those who are perishing, but to us who are being saved it is the power of God."

Likewise, God's weakness means God is seen weak when he cares for the weak. But in fact, God is stronger than human

---

8. Kim, *Messiah in Weakness*, 114–115.

strength as he chooses the foolish and the weak: "But God chose what is foolish in the world to shame the wise; God chose what is weak in the world to shame the strong; God chose what is low and despised in the world, things that are not, to reduce to nothing things that are" (1 Cor 1:27–28). As seen above, the cross includes the message of reversal and deconstruction of human wisdom and strength. All those who do not live according to God's true wisdom and strength are condemned. The message of the cross condemns all evil works and thoughts.

God's Justice on the Cross

On the cross of Jesus, God's justice (theodicy) is challenged. Where is God when Jesus is executed on the cross? What does Paul say about this issue? He resolves the issue of theodicy in two ways: God's vindication of Jesus by resurrecting him and God's final judgment in the future. In 1 Cor 13:4, he says that "he [Jesus] was crucified by (or from) weakness, but he lives by the power of God." His crucifixion by weakness connotes his powerlessness in the presence of Rome's violence against his teaching. His death seemed to be the end of the story from the eyes of Rome. But he lives by the power of God. That is, God's power resurrects Jesus from the dead. The message is that Jesus's death is not the end of the story. God vindicates him. He lives by God now. Nothing or no one can obstruct God's power. The fact that Jesus's life was taken, and that his body was broken is not the good news. But God responds to this "tragic, unjust" event by resurrecting him. God's kingdom does not require anyone to die. Rather, when God rules, all must live in justice and peace.

The other response to the problem of theodicy is to delay God's final judgment to the future. Paul deals with this issue in Rom 1:18—2:1–7. Now "the wrath of God is revealed from heaven against all ungodliness and wickedness of those who by their wickedness suppress the truth," and at the same time, God's righteousness is also revealed to those who live by faith (Rom 1:17). But the final day of the wrath of God is in the future, and until then, God is patient with them. This is because there is time for people to repent. Paul also warns against imperfect, often hypocritical, human judgments, as he states in Rom 2:1: "Therefore you have no excuse, whoever you are, when you judge others; for in passing judgment on another you condemn yourself, because you, the judge, are doing the very same things." He goes on to say in Rom 2:3-4: "Do you imagine, whoever you are, that when you judge those who do such things and yet do them yourself, you will escape the judgment of God? Or do you despise the riches of his kindness and forbearance and patience? Do you not realize that God's kindness is meant to lead you to repentance?" Here, Paul says that "you are not the judge, and that God will judge all in the future. Until then, your job is to live faithfully, honoring God's kindness and patience whose purpose is repentance." But he also ensures that there will be the day of wrath "when God's righteous judgment will be revealed" (Rom 2:5). On that day, God "will repay according to each one's deeds" (2:6).

Christ Crucified and the Gospel

Thus far we have variously explored the cause and meaning of Christ crucified. But all these explorations lead to Paul's gospel because, as he says in Rom 1:1, his apostolic calling is for "the good news of God." First, Christ crucified is not itself the gospel or good news (εὐαγγέλιον, *euangelion*). We need to remember that Paul's calling is for the gospel of God (Rom 1:1), and the good news of God means all good things about God. Therefore, apparently, Jesus's crucifixion is sad news to Christians and others who have sympathy for his death. In fact, there are no expressions or phrases like "the gospel of the cross" in the New Testament. Paul makes a distinction between the cross of Christ and the gospel, as he says in 1 Cor 1:17: "For Christ did not send me to baptize but to proclaim the gospel, and not with eloquent wisdom, so that the cross of Christ might not be emptied of its power." His aim is to proclaim the gospel to the Corinthians, not with eloquent wisdom but with the message (meaning and challenge) of the cross of Christ. In 1

Cor 1:17–31, he makes explicit about his message about the cross and presents an alternative wisdom and strength that are based on who God is and what he wants (1 Cor 1:25). For some, "the message about the cross is foolishness" because they do not understand, but those who understand correctly, it is the power of God (1 Cor 1:18). Thus he says in 1 Cor 1:23–24: "We proclaim Christ crucified, a stumbling block to Jews and foolishness to Gentiles, but to those who are the called, both Jews and Greeks, Christ the power of God and the wisdom of God" (1 Cor 1:23–24).

Otherwise, when Paul refers to the cross of Christ, he does so carefully. In Gal 6:12, responding to Jewish Christians who enforce Gentiles to be circumcised, he argues that Christ fought for freedom for all. The result is his death. Similarly, in Gal 6:14, he boasts about the cross of Jesus not because his death is good news but because it brings moral challenge to him: "May I never boast of anything except the cross of our Lord Jesus Christ, by which the world has been crucified to me, and I to the world." In Phil 3:18, Paul mentions those who oppose the gospel of Christ and calls "enemies of the cross of Christ." He warns against those who boast about their own identity or power without thinking about Christ's faith and his sacrifice for others. In sum, the cross of Christ is not itself good news or gospel. What Jesus did for God and the world constitutes the gospel of Christ. Through his outpouring love, God's righteousness has been manifested, and people can live a new life in the Spirit. That is the gospel of Christ. See below:

- 1 Corinthians 9:12: If others share this rightful claim on you, do not we still more? Nevertheless, we have not made use of this right, but we endure anything rather than put an obstacle in the way of the gospel of Christ.
- 2 Corinthians 2:12: When I came to Troas to proclaim the gospel of Christ, a door was opened for me in the Lord.
- 2 Corinthians 9:13: Through the testing of this ministry you glorify God by your obedience to the confession of the gospel of Christ and by the generosity of your sharing with them and with all others,

- 2 Corinthians 10:14: For we were not overstepping our limits when we reached you; we were the first to come all the way to you with the good news of Christ.

- Galatians 1:7: not that there is another gospel, but there are some who are confusing you and want to pervert the gospel of Christ.

- Romans 1:9: For God, whom I serve with my spirit by announcing the gospel of his Son, is my witness that without ceasing I remember you always in my prayers,

- Romans 15:19: by the power of signs and wonders, by the power of the Spirit of God, so that from Jerusalem and as far around as Illyricum I have fully proclaimed the gospel of Christ.

- 1 Thessalonians 3:2: and we sent Timothy, our brother and co-worker for God in proclaiming the gospel of Christ, to strengthen and encourage you for the sake of your faith.

- Philippians 1:27: Only, live your life in a manner worthy of the gospel of Christ, so that, whether I come and see you or am absent and hear about you, I will know that you are standing firm in one spirit, striving side by side with one mind for the faith of the gospel.

3

The Body of Christ at the Lord's Supper

IN THIS CHAPTER, WE will explore how Paul understands the Lord's supper tradition and how the body of Christ is related to it. In doing so, we will interpret the words of institution from a narrative approach. In fact, Paul is neither the eyewitness of Jesus's ministry nor his disciple; nevertheless, he says that he received the tradition about the Lord's supper from the Lord and delivered it to the Corinthians (1 Cor 11:23). This does not mean that he directly received this tradition from Jesus. The truth is that he never met Jesus in person. Rather, he was a persecutor of the church of God before he was called for the gospel of God (Gal 1:13; Acts 9:1–31). He became a follower of Jesus through the Christian story by other early Christian witnesses. From one community to another, from one person to another, stories about Jesus and his last meal were told again and again. Paul also received the tradition about Jesus and his last meal. In the process of storytelling, two elements are important: the received tradition and the storyteller's interpretation with necessary edits. Paul does the same thing here. He says he received the tradition about the Lord's supper and he handed it on to the Corinthians. In doing so, he must communicate both the kernel of the story and his interpretation of it in the Corinthian context. Through this narrative approach, we will explore the kernel story of the Lord's supper to which readers are transported back. For this job, we must focus on the context of Jesus's ministry and his work leading to the moment where he decides to have a farewell meal. Jesus's last meal with his disciples should be understood from the perspective of the story in that he reflects on his life and prepares for his gloomy future. We can neither separate this event from his life nor reduce it to a sacrificial sacrament for salvation. Rather, this event is a real story that creates many emotions: from thanksgiving to pain to memory. After this, we will explore Paul's interpretation of the last supper as he deals with the Corinthian community. He articulates the significance of a communal meal informed by Jesus's faith and his sacrifice.

The Kernel Story of the Lord's Supper

In the Synoptic Gospels, Jesus institutes the Lord's supper that is Passover meal. This event appears in Mark 14:22–25, Matt 26:26–29, and Luke 22:14–20, and its content is similar to one another because, according to the theory of Markan priority, Mark became a common literary source for Matthew and Luke. While Matthew changed it a bit, Luke did so much. However, the words of institution are fairly close to each other. That is, Jesus shares bread and wine and refers them to his body, saying he will never again have the same table until the kingdom of God is fulfilled. Though we do not know exactly what he said at this event, we can feel the kernel of this event from the Gospels and Paul's letters.

Mark 14:22–25
22 While they were eating, he took a loaf of bread, and after blessing it he broke it, gave it to them, and said, "Take; this is my body." 23 Then he took a cup, and after giving thanks he gave it to them, and all of them drank from it. 24 He said to them, "This is my blood of the covenant, which is poured out for many. 25 Truly I tell you, I will never again drink of the fruit of the vine until that day when I drink it new in the kingdom of God."

The Body of Christ at the Lord's Supper

Matthew 26:26-29
26 While they were eating, Jesus took a loaf of bread, and after blessing it he broke it, gave it to the disciples, and said, "Take, eat; this is my body." **27** Then he took a cup, and after giving thanks he gave it to them, saying, "Drink from it, all of you; **28** for this is my blood of the covenant, which is poured out for many for the forgiveness of sins. **29** I tell you, I will never again drink of this fruit of the vine until that day when I drink it new with you in my Father's kingdom."

Luke 22:14-20
14 When the hour came, he took his place at the table, and the apostles with him. **15** He said to them, "I have eagerly desired to eat this Passover with you before I suffer; **16** for I tell you, I will not eat it until it is fulfilled in the kingdom of God." **17** Then he took a cup, and after giving thanks he said, "Take this and divide it among yourselves; **18** for I tell you that from now on I will not drink of the fruit of the vine until the kingdom of God comes." **19** Then he took a loaf of bread, and when he had given thanks, he broke it and gave it to them, saying, "This is my body, which is given for you. Do this in remembrance of me." **20** And he did the same with the cup after supper, saying, "This cup that is poured out for you is the new covenant in my blood.

Paul also talks about the Lord's supper in 1 Corinthians 11:23–26, and the words of institution are close to the synoptic gospels. Also, in 1 Cor 10:16–21, he indirectly mentions the Lord's supper in dealing with the issue of food offered to idols. See 1 Cor 11:23–26 and 1 Cor 10:16–21:

1 Cor 11:23-26
23 For I received from the Lord what I also handed on to you, that the Lord Jesus on the night when he was betrayed took a loaf of bread, **24** and when he had given thanks, he broke it and said, "This

is my body that is for you. Do this in remembrance of me." **25** In the same way he took the cup also, after supper, saying, "This cup is the new covenant in my blood. Do this, as often as you drink it, in remembrance of me." **26** For as often as you eat this bread and drink the cup, you proclaim the Lord's death until he comes.

1 Cor 10:16–21
16 The cup of blessing that we bless, is it not a sharing in the blood of Christ? The bread that we break, is it not a sharing in the body of Christ? **17** Because there is one bread, we who are many are one body, for we all partake of the one bread. **18** Consider the people of Israel; are not those who eat the sacrifices partners in the altar? **19** What do I imply then? That food sacrificed to idols is anything, or that an idol is anything? **20** No, I imply that what pagans sacrifice, they sacrifice to demons and not to God. I do not want you to be partners with demons. **21** You cannot drink the cup of the Lord and the cup of demons. You cannot partake of the table of the Lord and the table of demons.

Paul's received tradition may be closer to the Lord's supper tradition than the gospels because 1 Corinthians (the mid-50's) predates the synoptic gospels (70–90 CE). Moreover, it seems that the Evangelists added their eschatological views to the meal event. Jesus's eschatological words that he will never have the same table reflect their concerns about the future. In other words, various groups of Christians in the first century CE believed that the Lord would return soon, and this belief is embedded in these eschatological sayings. But in 1 Cor 11:23–25 there are no eschatological sayings of Jesus. Rather, Paul, not Jesus, emphasizes the urgency of the last day: "For as often as you eat this bread and drink the cup, you proclaim the Lord's death until he comes" (1 Cor 11:26).

The mood of his last meal can be reconstructed through images and metaphors used in the event such as bread, wine, the new covenant, the body, and blood. But these images and metaphors must be understood in a larger narrative context. That is, they must be interpreted considering Jesus's ministry and his concern about the future. For example, in the narrative, Jesus provides not only bread but the word of God to the hungry and the poor. His concern about the future must be also realistic to this meal since he knows God's kingdom is yet to come. He knows he will be killed eventually if he does not stop proclaiming the gospel of God. But he submits to God's will and moves on with his message about God. When it comes to his last meal, he is ready to die for God and the world. Yet, he realizes that God's rule is still far away.

This narrative approach to Jesus's last meal is different from the traditional one in that only his death is emphasized. In this alternative approach to the Lord's supper, we do not limit our understanding to his death. Rather, at his last meal, he looks back to all he did and looks ahead the thorny road to Jerusalem. He knows there are not many days to live. At this last meal, he talks about his body and shares it with his disciples, asking them to remember him and his death.

At this last meal, Jesus takes a loaf of bread, gives thanks, breaks it and says: "This is my body that is for you. Do this in remembrance of me." In this text, there are a series of actions: "to take a loaf of bread, to give thanks to God, to break it, and to say words." First, "to take a loaf of bread" reminds readers of his work of feeding the five thousand in a desert and his teaching of God's word. "To give thanks to God" reminds readers of Jesus's attitude toward life. God is the source and sustainer of life. "To break bread" reminds them of his feeding of multitudes. Even five barley loaves are broken and shared to feed thousands of the hungry (John 6:1–14). Finally, he says: "This is my body that is for you. Do this in remembrance of me. This cup is the new covenant in my blood. Do this, as often as you drink it, in remembrance of me" (1 Cor 11:24–25). He says his body, like bread, is broken and given to his disciples. Obviously, this idea is weird because his body cannot be eaten. What he means is he served others through his life. In John's language, Jesus is "the living bread that came down from heaven," and he says: "Whoever eats of this bread will live forever; and the bread that I will give for the life of the world is my flesh"

(John 6:51). Similarly, in Mark 10:45, he says: "For the Son of Man came not to be served but to serve, and to give his life a ransom for many." "To give his life a ransom for many" can be understood as his lifelong work of God for the oppressed. Then, Jesus says: "Do this in remembrance of me." Remembering must be inclusive of all he did, including his death. Readers must remember all his joys, concerns, struggles, and death.

After this, Jesus takes the cup and says, "This cup is the new covenant in my blood. Do this, as often as you drink it, in remembrance of me." This saying has a similar structure to that of the bread. Both bread and wine refer to his life. That is, what he says is he served others and gave his life for all.

Retelling the Lord's Supper

Paul takes up the kernel story of the Lord's supper and retells it as if he were with Jesus and his disciples. In this vivid tradition, he and the Corinthians hear again what Jesus did to his disciples. They need to remember Jesus's life and his sacrifice again and again. But in the Corinthian church, the Lord's supper became an occasion of conflict because some members boast about their status and power. Some rich people came early to the supper and ate up all food without waiting for the other poor members (1 Cor 11:18–19). Paul is stern about them: "What! Do you not have homes to eat and drink in? Or do you show contempt for the church of God and humiliate those who have nothing? What should I say to you? Should I commend you? In this matter, I do not commend you!" (1 Cor 11:22). The irony is that the very place of union and harmony at the Lord's supper changes to a place of disunity because they did not follow the way of Christ. God wants a faithful community modeling after Jesus, as Paul says in 1 Cor 1:9–10: "God is faithful; by him you were called into the fellowship of his Son, Jesus Christ our Lord. Now I appeal to you, brothers and sisters, by the name of our Lord Jesus Christ, that all of you be in agreement and that there be no divisions among you, but that you be united in the same mind and the same purpose." They must follow Christ's mind and purpose, which is none other than glorifying God and revealing his righteousness.

To this divisive church, Paul reminds the Corinthians of the meaning of the Lord's supper and instructs them to do this: "For as often as you eat this bread and drink the cup, you proclaim the Lord's death until he comes" (1 Cor 11:26). Whenever they gather for the Lord's supper, they must remember Jesus's death and proclaim its message. Earlier in 1 Cor 1:17–18, Paul told them: "For Christ did not send me to baptize but to proclaim the gospel, and not with eloquent wisdom, so that the cross of Christ might not be emptied of its power. For the message about the cross is foolishness to those who are perishing, but to us who are being saved it is the power of God." Paul's charge is that the Corinthians must remember Jesus's holy sacrifice for God's righteousness.

Therefore, when Paul asks the Corinthians to proclaim the Lord's death at the Lord's supper, he means that they must remember his death and follow his faith. In 2 Cor 5:14, he says that because Jesus died for all, all have died. He does not say that because he died for all, all do not die. Paul says "I die every day" (1 Cor 15:31). Even baptism means dying with Christ, as in Rom 6:3: "Do you not know that all of us who have been baptized into Christ Jesus were baptized into his death?" To follow Christ, one must die with him and dares to die for God's righteousness. "Dying with Christ" means "to put to death the deeds of the body by the Spirit," and not "to live according to the flesh" (Rom 8:13). In the Corinthian context, "the deeds of the body" have to do with uncaring self-promotion ideologies and practices on the day of the Lord's supper. Some rich members bring their own food to the gathering place and eat up all without waiting for other poor members. Since a gathering at the Lord's supper is close to a Greco-Roman symposium, it may be possible that attendants did not sit at the same table. The rich members came early with their food and shared their table with other rich members. Other members came late and sat at a different table with no food to eat. Different tables may represent their social status and ideology.

Paul rebukes them because they do not understand the meaning of the Lord's supper. Paul's solution to the disunity of the community is to proclaim the Lord's death, which means to die with him. He clearly says in Gal 5:23 that "those who belong to Christ Jesus have crucified the flesh with its passions and desires." Membership in Christ does not depend on the knowledge about him but to die with him. Then they may bear the fruit of the Spirit: "love, joy, peace, patience, kindness, generosity, faithfulness, gentleness, and self-control" (Gal 5:22–23).

Ethical Exhortations

After retelling the story of the Lord's supper, Paul gives specific charges to the Corinthians in 1 Cor 11:27–34. On the one hand, he warns the Corinthians that they must attend the Lord's supper responsibly, and on the other hand, he is concerned about building a community of mutual care. He warns against the unworthy manner of taking the bread and the cup. First, they must know that the bread and the cup come from the same Lord, who laid the foundation of the church through faith. What needs to be shared among the Corinthians is Christ's holy sacrifice and his faith. His death must be proclaimed, and his faith must be followed when they share the bread and the cup. Second, all members must take the bread and the cup at the same time. Thus he says to them: "Wait for one another" (1 Cor 11:33). Therefore the unworthy manner means all thoughts and activities at the Lord's supper that are not informed by Christ's faith and his holy sacrifice.

Eventually, Paul's concern is how to build a community of mutual care and solidarity in Christ. For this task, he exhorts them to examine themselves and to discern the body (1 Cor 11:28–29). "Examining themselves and discerning the body" are interchangeable because both require them to act responsibly in community. At the Lord's supper, they must know why they come together, who comes late or who is hungry, or who is sitting next to them. Their thought and action must cohere in the manner that they honor Christ's life. All they do must be rooted in Christ, in his faith, so that they may glorify God in their body (1 Cor 6:20). They also must put to death sinful passions and desires of the flesh. They "were called into the fellowship (koinonia) of his Son, Jesus" (1 Cor 1:9). Koinonia means "to share in" or "to participate." They were invited to the Lord's supper to share in Jesus's faith and his life. His body and blood is a symbol of his presence among the members. Thus they have to be united in the same mind of Christ.

Likewise, in 1 Cor 8:1—11:1, Paul exhorts the Corinthians to think and act in the spirit of Jesus. Since they share in the body of Christ and the blood of Christ, they have to follow him (1 Cor 10:16). In other words, they should not boast about their knowledge or power (1 Cor 10:23). Likewise, he goes on to say: "Do not seek your own advantage, but that of the other" (1 Cor 10:24; cf. 1 Cor 6:12); "So, whether you eat or drink, or whatever you do, do everything for the glory of God. Give no offense to Jews or to Greeks or to the church of God, just as I try to please everyone in everything I do, not seeking my own advantage, but of many, so that they may be saved" (1 Cor 10:31–33). Likewise, regarding sexual immorality (1 Cor 6:12–20), the real problem is some do not discern their bodies and sleep with a prostitute. The issue is more than that of fornication. It has more to do with embodiment of Christ, as he says: "Or do you not know that your body is a temple of the Holy Spirit within you, which you have from God, and that you are not your own? For you were bought with a price; therefore glorify God in your body" (1 Cor 6:19–20). The Corinthians are "members of Christ" and therefore they are to be united to him, in agreement with his spirit and faith. Here "members" are *mele* in Greek and refers to body parts, not referring to members of society in an organism sense. That is, the Corinthians, as body parts of Christ, should be united to the Lord and become "one spirit with him" (1 Cor 6:17). In contrast, those who are united to a prostitute become one spirit with her. So the issue is where one is united.

4

The Body of Christ and the Community

TRADITIONALLY, "THE BODY OF Christ" in 1 Cor 12:12–27 and Rom 12:4–5 has been understood as a metaphor for an organism, especially based on the *homonoia* speeches in Stoicism. In this reading, what is emphasized is unity of the church whose head is Christ. But this reading can be challenged by an alternative reading that understands the body of Christ as a metaphor for a way of living.[1] Namely, what Paul emphasizes to the community is not merely a lack of unity but a disembodiment of Christ. In the traditional interpretation, "the body of Christ" in 1 Cor 12–27 and Rom 12:4–5 has been understood as a unified community in Christ. That is, the body was understood as a community (metaphorical organism) and the purpose of the metaphor is unity. Certainly, this unity reading is very plausible given the fact that Stoic ideal of unity (*homonoia*) may have been adopted by Paul. Stoicism views the human body as a bound system of a hierarchy. For example, the head is a most important part, and other parts have to serve it. With this hierarchical view of the body, Stoics emphasize the unity of society that is viewed as a hierarchical body, requiring different social classes to work together without complaints. The implication is the lower classes are sacrificed in the name of oneness or unity. In this view, unity becomes a rhetoric of control of the

---

1. Kim, *Christ's Body in Corinth*, 65–96.

weak and marginalized. Unity becomes an ideology of the ruling class. The content of unity is packed with nice propaganda such as Roman peace and security. But Paul does not accept this kind of hierarchical unity by Stoicism; rather, he argues all parts of the body are important and respected even though they are different in their abilities or social status. The different parts of the body do different works, and yet they are not hierarchically structured.

In an alternative interpretation of "the body of Christ," we can perceive of "the body" as a metaphor for a way of living. That is, the body is a site of living. In this alternative view, the issue in the Corinthian church or Roman church is not a mere lack of unity but a lack of diversity. In this view, the human body is understood differently, not as a bound system of a hierarchy but as a system of solidarity. For this alternative reading, first of all, we need to explore the difference between unity and union. Then, we will explore "the body of Christ" in 1 Cor 12:12–27 and Rom 12:4–5 from a perspective of union. Finally, we will see what the Corinthians and Roman Christians have to do to stay in union with Christ. In this alternative reading, Paul is very critical of four divisions in the Corinthian community (a party belonging to Paul; to Apollos; to Cephas; and to Christ, as in 1 Cor 1:11) because they do not care for the weak or the marginalized. Even though details about these four factions are unknown to us, one thing is certain they do not stand on the foundation of the church, which is Christ.

"Rigid" Unity or "Soft" Union

Unity means the state of being in full agreement, which echoes the rhetoric of homonoia (concord) by Stoics. Roman rulers say that society is one body and that all members have to work hard in their place without complaining or asking for a change in the patron-client system. All members of society are required to speak the same language of unity, which is, in fact, the language of control by the Roman Empire. Unity or oneness is used by the rulers to maintain a hierarchical society. The Emperor is the head of the body, controlling the whole body, speaking for them, interpreting what unity means for them. In this state of imperial unity, diversity is inconceivable because the center (the norm) dominates discourse for all members, who cannot voice their ideas freely.

Now the question is: Does Paul use this above concept of unity when he talks about the Corinthian community in 1 Cor 12? The answer is no because his view of the community is egalitarian. According to Paul, the Corinthians are free in Christ, doing God's work freely because of the gifts of the Spirit. Men and women are equally partnered in their ministry. Women pray and prophesy in the church, speaking tongues. In other words, diversity infuses the Corinthian church. So he does not seem to think that the Corinthians must sing in unison or in full agreement with each other. In Paul's church, there is no head or center of the body. The body is one but there is no hierarchy in it. Even the head is a part of the body. All parts are equally treated with respect and protection because that is what the body means from the perspective of union. At Corinth, the marginalized and the weak are lifted up because they are also parts of the body. All parts should be united/connected with Christ, who is not the church or its head but the locus of living in a union. Paul never refers Christ to the church directly in 1 Corinthians and elsewhere in the seven undisputed letters. God is the owner of the church.

So Paul's concept of the body as a community is close to the concept of union. "Union" generally means "an act of joining two or more things together," which emphasizes the state of being together.[2] In a realistic sense, the Corinthian community is better

---

2. The Merriam Webster Dictionary. Accessed on August 17, 2016. http://www.merriam-webster.com/dictionary/union. In biblical or Pauline theology, union with Christ is understood along with the concept of "in Christ," which appears frequently in Paul's letters. "In Christ" or "union with Christ" is understood variously: (1) as membership in the church ("in Christ" as spatial relationships); (2) as salvation or justification ("in Christ" as instrumental relationships); (3) as Christ's mystic presence with an individual ("in Christ" as temporal relationships; (4) as the manner of life ("in Christ" as modal relationships). In view of the history of interpretation, the first three understandings of "in Christ" have been dominant. For example, regarding the understanding (1), "only in the Lord" in 1 Cor 7:39 ("A wife is bound as long as her husband lives. But if the husband dies, she is free to marry anyone she wishes, *only in*

compared to this union because many different members, coming from different backgrounds in their social status, are gathered together to live a common religious life. When gathered together, they actually have more differences than commonalities.

But the actual community does not function like this ideal union because some members try to dominate other members or the entire community. To deal with all kinds of issues that divide the community, Paul, taking up the image of the human body, explains the ideal nature of the community united with Christ. In the body, all parts are connected with one another, suffering and rejoicing together. If one part suffers, the whole body also suffers. The ancient Greek physician Hippocrates well observes about this in *Places in Man*:[3]

> 1.1 In my view, there is no beginning in the body; but everything is alike beginning and end. For when a circle has been drawn, its beginning is not to be found.
>
> 1.4 The body is homogenous (lit. the same as itself) and is composed of the same things, though not in uniform

---

the Lord") has been interpreted through the sense of boundary marker; that is, the advice is to marry another Christian. See Tertullian, *Against Marcion* 5.7; Jerome, *Epistles* 123.5; Calvin, *First Epistle* 168. See also Rudolf Bultmann, *The Theology of the New Testament*, Vol. 1. trans. Kendrick Grobel (New York, NY: Charles Scribner's Sons, 1951), 309-11; Günter Bornkamn, *Paul*, trans. D.M.G. Stalker (New York, NY: Harper & Row, 1971), 155. Regarding the understanding (2), see C.H. Dodd, *The Epistle of Paul to the Romans* (New York, NY: R. Long & R. R. Smith, 1931), 87; Fritz Neugebauer, "Das Paulinische 'in Christo," *New Testament Studies* 4 (1957-58): 124-38. Regarding the understanding (3), see Adolf Deissmann, *Paul: A Study in Social and Religious History*, trans. William E. Wilson (London: Hodder and Stoughton, 1926), 113-92; Albert Schweitzer, *The Mysticism of Paul the Apostle*, trans. William Montgomery (Baltimore: John Hopkins University Press, 1998), 380-88. Regarding the understanding (4), see Ernst Käsemann, *Perspectives on* Paul, trans. Margaret Kohl (Philadelphia, PA: Fortress, 1971), 102-21. For an overall review of "in Christ" scholarship, see A.J.M. Wedderburn, "Some Observations on Paul's Use of the Phrase 'in Christ' and 'with Christ," *Journal for the Study of the New Testament* 25 (1985): 83-97.

3. Hippocrates, *Places in Man*, trans. Elizabeth Craik (Oxford: Clarendon Press, 1998), 37-39.

disposition, in its small parts and its large; in parts above and parts below. And if you like to take the smallest part of the body and injure it, the whole body will feel the injury, whatever sort it may be, for this reason, that the smallest part of the body has all the things that the biggest part has.

1.5 This smallest part refers to its own entity whatever it may experience, whether it be bad or good. And for this reason the body feels pain or pleasure from its smallest constituent because all parts exist in the smallest part and these refer everything to each of their own related parts, and register everything.

Though there is no evidence that Paul read Hippocrates, one thing must be clear that Hippocrates' medical knowledge and insights were influential to subsequent generations. In fact, Paul's body talks in 1 Cor 12:12–26 is similar to the Hippocratic tradition where the human body is understood through union or connection of all parts in one body, rather than through the unity of one body. Horden captures this point well: "Granted, to feel pain, in general, is, for the Hippocratics, part of the human condition. We feel pain because, as the Nature of Man has it, we are not a unity. If we are made up entirely of one element, pain could be impossible, for unity would not exhibit change and corruption, excess and deficiency, and these, as we read in Places in Man, are the causes of pain." The Hippocratic writers are positive about curing diseases through seeking "fine balance" in the body. Apparently, Paul's body analogy in 1 Cor 12:12–26 implies this importance of balancing among members. Parts of the body look different and work differently, but they are a connected whole, working voluntarily for the body, not being commanded by the center. In the same body, all parts are respected and taken good care of. This connectedness and equal care with all parts differ from the hegemonic body politic of the Roman society.

The idea of "union with Christ" is also expressed in 1 Cor 6:12–20. Challenging the sexually immoral persons, Paul charges the Corinthians to be united with Christ, not with the prostitutes because they were bought with a price and their body is a temple of the Holy Spirit (1 Cor 6:19–20). The right place of their union is Christ through whom they have to glorify God in their body. So he asks, "Do you not know that your bodies are parts (μέλη) of Christ? Should I therefore take the parts (μέλη) of Christ and make them parts (μέλη) of a prostitute? Never!" (1 Cor 6:15). Here the Greek μέλη is the plural noun of μέλος, which means a body part. The issue is where they are united. Once they are united with somebody, they have to follow the mind of somebody: "Do you not know that whoever is united to a prostitute becomes one body with her?" (1 Cor 6:16). Paul answers: "But anyone united to the Lord becomes one spirit with him" (1 Cor 6:17). "One spirit with him" means to follow the way of his life. Union with Christ requires the Corinthians to use their body responsibly in building a community of love and solidarity with the marginalized.

The Body of Christ as a Metaphor for Living

In 1 Cor 12:12–27, Paul talks about the human body as an analogy.[4] In the human body, many different parts are united with the body. All parts, both more honorable and less honorable are united in joy and suffering, and work together for the good of the body. For if one part is out of alignment, then the whole body is not aligned or in good order. All parts are equally important and taken care of. That is what Paul says in 1 Cor 12:12a: "For just as the body

---

4. Similarly, in Rom 12:4–5, Paul says: "For as in one body we have many members, and not all the members have the same function, so we, who are many, are one body in Christ, and individually we are members one of another." This passage, like 1 Cor 12:12–27, has been read as a unified community in Christ. But with a different notion of the body, that is, through the perspective of union or a metaphor for a way of living, we can understand Rom 12:4–5 differently. Here, the body is not a social body but the human body as a system of solidarity. He says that the body has many parts but it is one body in Christ. One body can be understood as union with Christ; that is, Roman Christians have to be united with Christ and follow his faith and his life. "In Christ" may be also understood in view of a modal dative, pointing to the Christ-like manner of life.

is one and has many members." In 1 Cor 12:12, it must be noted that Paul eventually applies this kind of "one body" to Christ: "and all members of the body, though many, are one body, so it is with Christ." The Corinthians as a whole constitute a body (like the human body), which is Christ. In this reading, the point is not that the community is a body (in the sense of organism) but that Christ is the body with which the Corinthians are to be united. In that union, there is a sense of "one body" that "if one member suffers, all suffer together with it; if one member is honored, all rejoice together with it" (1 Cor 12:26). In this reading of union, "the body of Christ" in 1 Cor 12:27 is understood as a site of living and the whole verse will be translated as follows: "You (the Corinthians) are the Christic body and you have to embody it individually and communally." "The Christic body" is an attributive genitive (another example in Rom 6:6: "the body of sin" as "the sin-ruled body.)" Usually, "the body of Christ" has been understood through a metaphorical organism in that the body represents a community (the church) belonging to Christ. But with this alternative understanding of the body—the body as a site of life, the whole meaning of 12:27 changes. If the Corinthians are parts of the body (Christ), they have to be united with him, remaining in his teaching, following the way of his life.

From Paul's perspective, the deeper issue is not a mere conflict among different factions but a dissolution of the whole body because some were detached from Christ and did not follow the way of Christ. The Corinthian community must include and embrace the most unfortunate in society (1 Cor 1:26–31). Both the strong and the weak are to constitute the community, all being equally respected because of God, who called them into the fellowship of his Son (1 Cor 1:9). Nothing or nobody can define the Corinthian community other than through God or his Son. Leaders of the church must be servants of God; they are not representatives of God as if they had special power or privilege. There is a division of labor, but no one can do it all. Paul says all members belong to God, not to Christ (1 Cor 3:22). God is the beginning and source of life in Christ, who witnesses to the good news of God (1 Cor

1:30; cf. Rom 1:11. In this ideal community of union with Christ, women are not subordinate to men. No particular doctrine or teaching can be a norm other than the way of Christ. This ideal community is stated in Gal 3:28: "There is no longer Jew or Greek, there is no longer slave or free, there is no longer male and female; for all of you are one in Christ Jesus." "All of you are one in Christ" is a summary statement of the perfect union with Christ. They are one not because they think or act the same but they are united with Christ, who is the foundation of the church, as Paul says in 1 Cor 3:11: "For no one can lay any foundation other than the one that has been laid; that foundation is Jesus Christ."

However, when different people gather together, they compete or boast about what they have. Some exercise excessive individualistic freedom in Christ. They attempt to control the community through their social status or other forms of power such as knowledge or wealth. The disunited members have to come back to "the way of Christ." First, the Corinthians must have a new perspective on life, seeking to appreciate God's foolishness and weakness. Instead of seeking splendid power or honor, they must see the grace of God in the presence of the marginalized and the weak. A wise person is not someone who knows much about the world and other people, but the one who knows he/she is nothing before God (1 Cor 4:10–13). Paul says he is nothing in 1 Cor 15:9–10: "For I am the least of the apostles, unfit to be called an apostle, because I persecuted the church of God. But by the grace of God I am what I am, and his grace toward me has not been in vain. On the contrary, I worked harder than any of them—though it was not I, but the grace of God that is with me." Similarly, in 1 Cor 4:10–13, he responds to those "wise persons in Christ" with the acknowledgment that he is nothing because of God's ministry.

Second, those who have this perspective of foolishness and weakness always must be informed by "the cross of Christ" (1 Cor 1:17) because otherwise, they are not worthy to be called saints (1 Cor 1:2). "The cross of Christ" is highlighted in an inverted parallelism between 1 Cor 1:1–9 and 1:10–17. The former is a section emphasizing the calling of the Corinthians and their membership to "the church of God" (1 Cor 1:1–9), and the latter is a section emphasizing the cross of Christ, which reveals the power of God. The cross of Christ is the basis that the Corinthians must be "in the same mind and the same purpose" as he says in 1 Cor 1:10: "Now I appeal to you, brothers and sisters, by the name of our Lord Jesus Christ, that all of you be in agreement and that there be no divisions among you, but that you be united in the same mind and the same purpose." Here "the same mind and the same purpose" must be understood from the perspective of union, where all parts share the same vision of Christ toward a hopeful future in God. Because they are united with Christ, they must share a common destiny with one another, suffering and rejoicing together. Their ultimate hope is the transformation of life in God. Having the same mind does not mean that the Corinthians must agree in all matters of their community life, thinking and acting in full agreement with others. Rather, he urges them to think and act through the mind of Christ, which is seen clearly in his cross because of his sacrificial love for the marginalized. When united with the cross of Christ, they can all participate in the power of God with one mind.

Third, the Corinthians should not seek their own advantage, but that of the other, as Paul says in 1 Cor 11:24. Though they are free in Christ, they are also free not to do something. To those exercising excessive freedom and practicing objective knowledge, he says "all things are lawful, but not all things are beneficial" (1 Cor 6:12; 10:23). To the proto-Gnostic believers in Corinth who argue the body does not matter, being involved in sexual immorality, he says the body matters because it is "a temple of the Holy Spirit" (1 Cor 6:19). To those who freely eat meat offered to idols, he says knowledge puffs up, but love builds up (1 Cor 8:1).

Fourth, similarly, they should not judge others in the community (1 Cor 4:1–16). When they do not examine their own minds and hearts, they look for others to find fault. So Paul says: "Do not pronounce judgment before the time, before the Lord comes, who will bring to light the things now hidden in darkness and will disclose the purpose of the heart" (1 Cor 4:5). They must examine themselves and focus on their ministry given by Jesus. One way they can examine themselves is to search for the Holy Spirit, which "searches everything, even the depths of God" (1 Cor 2:10).

5

Reclaiming Christ's Body for the Embodiment of God's Gospel[1]

I AM CONCERNED THAT the significance of "the body of Christ" in Paul's letters has been glossed over by the later Pauline letters such as Ephesians or Colossians.[2] In the latter, it is clear that the body of Christ is used as a metaphorical organism: "for the sake of *his body*, that is, the church *(ekklesia)*" (Col 1:18,24; Eph 1:22–23). We see here that Christ's body is the church, whose head is Christ. Paul's letters have been read through this metaphorical lens. For example, 1 Cor 12:27 ("you are the body of Christ") is understood as: "You, members, constitute Christ's body (as a social body)."

The primary weakness of this metaphorical reading lies in the fact that there is no clear articulation of how members can be

---

1. My earlier published article, Yung Suk Kim, "Reclaiming Christ's Body *(soma christou)*: Embodiment of God's Gospel in Paul's Letters," *Interpretation* 67.1 (2013): 20–29, is reused in this chapter with a revised title. Thanks go to *Interpretation: A Journal of Bible and Theology*.

2. The traditional Pauline letters are divided into three groups: 1) the seven undisputed letters (Romans, 1–2 Corinthians, Galatians, 1 Thessalonians, Philippians, and Philemon); 2) Deutero-Pauline letters (Colossians, Ephesians, and 2 Thessalonians); 3) Pastoral letters (1–2 Timothy, Titus). Scholars debate the authorship of the last two groups. The main reason for later non-Pauline authorship is that there are different writing styles, vocabulary, theology, and issues. In this article, Paul's letters refer to the seven undisputed letters.

united with Christ.³ In my reading, the body of Christ in 1 Cor 12:27 can be read as Christ's own body, Christ's body crucified, or Christ-like life: "You have to live like Christ." In other words, it can be read as a metaphor for "a way of living." Here, the body represents the location of living. It is not the same as a community or the church. Similarly, the body of Christ in Rom 7:4 ("dying to the law through the body of Christ") refers to Christ's body crucified or his life and death. If we read the body of Christ this way, then unity of the community is achieved and maintained not by Christ but by following the way of Christ—a way of association with Christ crucified.

Throughout his letters, Paul emphasizes the very Christ crucified, broken, and sacrificed, which is the central key to understanding Paul's theology. Paul says in 1 Cor 2:2: "For I decided to know nothing among you except Jesus Christ, and him crucified." Christ crucified is the one who brings "God's gospel" to the world (Rom 1:1–6). In Paul's letters, God's gospel is interchangeable with God's righteousness, and Christ as the Son of God shows his faith to reveal God's righteousness in the world (Rom 3:21–22). In Paul's theology, therefore, the believer's job is to imitate Christ (1 Cor 4:16; 11:1). Likewise, Paul's theology involves three parts: God's gospel or righteousness, Christ's faith (shown in his life and death), and the believer's participation in Christ's faith.⁴ In fact, this way of understanding Paul's theology is well stated in Rom 1:1 ("Paul, a slave of Jesus Christ, called to be an apostle, set apart for the gospel of God") and Rom 3:22 ("God's righteousness through Jesus Christ's faith for all who have faith").

The Body in Context: The Greco-Roman World and Paul

In the Greco-Roman world, Stoics promote the hierarchical, hegemonic body politic in which the elite or the strong rule the weak or

---

3. Kim, *Christ's Body in Corinth*, 1–9.
4. Kim, *A Theological Introduction to Paul's Letters*, 15–37.

the lower class. In this body politic, slaves must serve the superiors not simply because they are weak or powerless but because their destiny is to serve their lords. Likewise, hierarchical unity is granted, becoming a norm of society. However, we cannot assume that the marginalized easily accept this dominant social philosophy of the strong. As Roman comedies or satires express, slaves and the devastated bodies in society shout for a change for a better world.[5] Through theatrical forms, slaves demonstrate the desperate need for justice. At times, they protest the brutal system of society. Often, Cynic philosophers deride the power of the elites. All this is clearly a voice of protest against the dominant body politic based in hegemonic unity.

Against this backdrop, Paul does not seem to support the hegemonic body politic sponsored by Stoicism. Rather, he reverses the social convention of the hierarchical body or hierarchical unity in Stoicism, as he says that the weakest part of the body receives honor. In society, the weak must serve the strong, and honor is given to those at the top of society. But in Paul's community, honor is given to all, not by social status but by God's radical love and justice. All in Paul's community are equal partners of God's church. We also see Paul eloquently advocating solidarity of the community in Christ in 1 Corinthians. In Corinth, as in the other big cities of the Roman Empire, there are voiceless, landless, nameless, poor people. In fact, the majority of the Corinthian church comes from the lower class (1 Cor 1:26–30). While the bodies of the elite and strong males are greatly admired, the lowly bodies in society are despised or uncared for. Paul faces many marginalized people in Corinth in his ministry—bodies broken both physically and psychologically. Paul may have cried: "Wretched man that I am! Who will rescue me from this body of death?" (Rom 7:24). Where is God in the midst of total devastation of the weak bodies? In this situation, Paul communicates God's love to them through the image of Christ crucified. First, Christ's death is the sign of

---

5. Kim, *Christ's Body in Corinth*, 39–54. See also Larry Welborn, *Paul, the Fool of Christ: A Study of 1 Corinthians 1—4 in the Cosmic-Philosophic Tradition* (London: T & T Clark, 2005), 36.

God's love; he was killed because of his radical love of God for the most vulnerable. Christ's body was broken and crucified as a result of his embodiment of God's gospel— the cost of embracing the weak, the powerless, and the marginalized. Second, the resurrection of Christ is the sign of God's victory and judgment against the evildoers. So the followers of Jesus will be hopeful now and forever because of God's power. They will be transformed into the "spiritual body" (1 Cor 15:44).[6]

If Christ's body is re-imagined through the broken bodies in the world, and if God vindicates and resurrects Christ because of Christ's bold act of love and justice, then there is hope for those who follow Christ Jesus, because God will vindicate them too. So Paul decides to follow Christ in every way possible in his life and death: "Being crucified with Christ" (Gal 2:20; 1 Cor 2:2); "Dying on a cross everyday" (1 Cor 15:31); "Baptized into Christ's death" (Rom 6:3); "Die and rise" (Rom 6:6–11); "Put to death the deeds of the flesh" (Rom 8:13); and "Submit to God's law" (Rom 8:7). With this alternative reading of the body in contexts, we may ask ourselves: "What if we were Christ's broken body in the world? What if we were those broken bodies in the world?" Can we break our hearts for those who need a life of liberation and freedom? How can we participate in Christ's body, in his life and death?

Who is Paul? What Caused Him to Change?

In order to understand Paul's view of the body, it is worth noting the change of his view of God, the Messiah, and the world. Before his new experience with Christ, Paul sees that God is a Jewish God who made a covenant with Jews. Because of this view of God, Paul persecuted Christian gatherings. But now he realizes that this same God is the God of both Jews and Gentiles. This

---

6. In terms of Paul's theology, the cross of Jesus takes center stage. Resurrection is a logical result of Christ's faith that risks his life. Paul always emphasizes that Christian job is not done yet and Christians have to suffer until the final victory of God in the future (cf. 1 Cor 15:12–28; Gal 2:19–20; Phil 1:20–21, 29; 2 Cor 1:8–11; 12:9–10; Rom 8:16–17).

same covenant now extends to all. This is a radical change, because traditionally only the Jews are the covenant partners. Covenant partnership now extends to all, according to Paul, through the Messiah, Christ crucified, which is a scandal to the Greeks and blasphemy to the Jews. But Paul realizes that Christ crucified is evidence of both God's love and God's judgment. Christ's death is the result of his obedience to the love of God that embraces the poor and the marginalized. At the same time, Christ's death is an expression of God's judgment against those who participate in evil.

With this change of Paul's view of God and the Messiah, the way of transformation of the world also changes. Formerly, Paul believed that the world could be hopeful only through the Jewish tradition, a way of rigid observance of Jewish laws and customs, as shown in his zeal for the law and God.⁷ Now Paul realizes that the hope of the world is possible through the way of Christ crucified, a new Messiah who exemplifies God's love in/for the world (1 Cor 1:18—4:21). Paul also realizes that the true wisdom or knowledge of God has to do with restoration of the weak and the downcast in society. God's wisdom is not like the wisdom of the world that privileges the strong and the powerful at the expense of the lower class.

All these changes in Paul can be summarized in his threefold gospel that balances the roles of God, Christ, and the followers.⁸ First, Paul's gospel is theocentric. God is the source and actor of the gospel (good news), which is promised through "his prophets in the holy scriptures" (Rom 1:2). Second, Christ's faith manifests God's righteousness in the world (Rom 3:21–22). The gospel concerns Christ's work (Rom 1:3). Christ severs God! Third, believers participate with Christ (or Christ's death) through faith. As a

---

7. Paul's view of the law is not legalistic or pessimistic because of the law's inability to grant salvation to humans. Rather, the problem is their misuse of the law or zeal about it. Otherwise, the law is perfect and holy. The serious, fundamental problem of humans is that people indulge in self-promotion or honor at the sacrifice of others. For Paul, Christ is the goal of the law (Rom 10:4). Love fulfills the whole law (Gal 5:14).

8. Kim, *A Theological Introduction to Paul's Letters*, 15–37.

result, God's righteousness can be manifested continually in the world (Rom 3:22).

The Body Metaphor in Paul's Letters

In fact, Paul's theology of Christ crucified is not made in a vacuum. As we see in Corinth, Paul's churches are full of problems, ranging from sexual immorality to communal eating. All these problems boil down to a fundamental issue regarding the body. That is, members of the community do not remember and reflect Christ-like body, his sacrifice and love for others. Instead, people seek their own power or status at the expense of others. So, there is division in the Corinthian community. There are many broken bodies and souls in the community and outside of it. Suddenly, the costly love of God is forgotten and Christ's bodily sacrifice is exchanged for individualistic, self-seeking glory. This picture is, more or less, what we see at Corinth. In fact, this kind of problem pervades Paul's congregations. That is why we see the image of the body permeated throughout his letters, especially in 1–2 Corinthians, Galatians, and Romans. First Corinthians is a good example, in which Paul exhorts the Corinthians to live like Christ, not simply because they are one in Christ but because they are parts of Christ crucified.

Because of the vast array of the community problems in Corinth, Paul uses the body metaphor, not as an organism metaphor (e.g., such as seen in Col 1:18 or Eph 1:22–24), but as a metaphor for a way of living, Christ's bodily sacrifice for bringing the gospel of God. There is an urgent need for addressing these issues and exhorting the Corinthians to follow Christ, especially in his faith and other-centered love because of God's gospel. Not surprisingly, therefore, we see in Paul's letters that the body of Christ (*soma christou*) is distinguished from the church (*ekklesia*). First of all, Paul never puts *soma christou* ("the body of Christ") side by side with *ekklesia* (which simply means a community) in his seven letters. Whenever referring to the church, Paul uses the phrase "the church of God" (1 Cor 1:2; 10:32; 11:22; 15:9; 2 Cor 1:1; Gal

1:13), not "the church of Christ." Christ obeyed the law of God for God's household to which all people may belong.

Second, in 1 Corinthians, what is being built in fact is not *soma christou* ("the body of Christ") but *ekklesia* (the church) as an institution (1 Cor 14:4). It is in Deutero-Pauline letters that Christ's body is used as an organism ("Christ is the head of the *ekklesia*, *his body*" in Eph 5:22; "for the sake of *his body*, that is, *ekklesia*" in Col 1:24; "building up of the body of Christ" in Eph 4:12).[9] In these Deutero-Pauline letters, *mele* (parts of the human body) clearly refers to social members as in a metaphorical organism: "We are members of his body" (Eph 5:30; cf. Eph 3:6; Col 3:15).

Third, in 1 Corinthians, "the body of Christ" is not an object but a predicate nominative: "You are Christ's body" (1 Cor 12:27).[10] The significance of Paul's language here is that "you" are agents of carrying the life of Christ. Similarly, "You are God's temple" (1 Cor 3:16; cf. 6:19). What this implies for Paul is that the body of Christ as a metaphor is too important to apply to an organism. Simply, Christ's body symbolizes Christ's sacrifice, his life, and death. Then, combined with the subject "you," the believers are associated with Christ's body. Therefore, now the meaning of 1 Cor 12:27a can be: "You are Christ's body; you are Christ-like body." Lastly, in 1 Corinthians 12 the word *ekklesia* (church) does not appear until 12:28. In 1 Cor 12:12–27, Paul explains what the community should look like—it should model Christ as a focus. Members should treat each other like parts *(mele)* of Christ's own body.[11] After this, Paul uses the word *ekklesia* (church) in 1

---

9. The equation of the body and the church is found in Eph 1:22—23 and Col 1:18. However, during Paul's ministry he does not have so much concern over administrative matters of the church partly because end-time is near and mainly because his radical theology of *Christic* embodiment is more important than anything else. It is believed that only in a much later time that students of Paul co-opt for social hierarchy and church management the use of a metaphorical organism: so now the church is "the body of Christ," an institution, whose head is Christ.

10. Kim, *Christ's Body in Corinth*, 65–95.

11. In the next section, we will see more about *mele* (parts). Here *mele* refers to human body parts. The idea is that believers have to consider themselves attached to Christ's body (as human body), not to a social body.

Cor 12:28: "In the church, God has appointed first apostles." This implies that Paul makes a distinction between Christ's body (as a body analogy) and the church (as an institution).

Why is it so important to distinguish between *soma christou* and *ekklesia* in Paul's letters? The answer is as follows: If we take Paul's use of *soma christou* as Christ's own body or Christ's life and death, then the metaphor of Christ's body has redemptive and corrective purposes for the world. As a redemptive purpose, Christ's body symbolizes Christ's sacrifice, his solidarity with the broken and vulnerable bodies in the world. As a corrective purpose, Christ's body represents a protest against all dominant systems that subjugate the weak bodies. *Ekklesia* (the church) is a result of Christ's embodiment of God's gospel and the believers' ongoing participation in his death. The church is an ongoing institution (organism) that continues to participate in Christ's life and death. Conversely, if the body of Christ is solely understood as a social body (metaphorical organism), then there may be a tendency for church members to believe that only they are God's people and to treat people outside the church as no-bodies or hopeless people. However, in Paul's theology God is in charge of everything, and such a God is merciful enough and inclusive enough for all people. Paul confesses that God's wisdom and knowledge is too deep and mysterious to be measured by humans (Rom 11:33–36). Therefore, no one can judge people on the basis of their conditions of life, as we know from Romans 9–11, where Paul vehemently defends God's freedom and love toward the place of Israel and Gentiles. In the following, we will look into various aspects of Christ's body that refer to Christ's faith, sacrifice, and life.

Christ's Body as a Metaphor of Holism

The community of Christ (the church) continues its function only when the members of the community live like Christ. It is modeled after Christ's faith and his life examples that continue to provide rationale and support for the community. We look into the following two texts to see the holistic concept of the body in the Corinthian community.

1 Corinthians 6:15–20

In 1 Cor 6:15-20, Paul asks: "Do you not know that your bodies are members of Christ? Should I therefore take the members of Christ and make them members of a prostitute?" The NRSV translates the Greek noun *mele* as "members" as if *mele* refers to social members of a community. But in ordinary sense, *mele* more directly refers to parts of the human body, not members of a social body.[12] Therefore, the issue is whether one can live worthily as a part of Christ's body. In other words, the challenge to the Corinthians is "how to use the body." If united with Christ, the Corinthians are to live like a worthy part of Christ. They cannot take parts of Christ and make them into parts of a prostitute (1 Cor 6:15). The reason for their holy living is that "your body is the temple of the Spirit" (1 Cor 6:19) and also "you were bought with a price" (1 Cor 7:23). Here "a price" means Christ's sacrifice for God's gospel—a cost of embodiment of God's righteousness. The object of purchase is "your body" or "you." So you "do not become slaves of human masters" (1 Cor 7:23). Christ's sacrifice is not a price that guarantees their identity or salvation once and for all, nor does it replace the cost of embodying God's love. The only thing the Corinthians should do is to glorify God in everyday lives (1 Cor 6:20).

1 Corinthians 12:12–27

In 1 Cor 12:12—27, the body is a litmus test that members of the community should feel connected and united. When one part of the body suffers, the whole body suffers. In this passage the key message is mutual care and respect in a community, which is possible not because the community is one like a social body of a Stoic

---

12. The most recent English translation, *The Common English Bible*, translates *mele* as "parts."

metaphor *(homonoia* speech), but because community members are equal partners of God's church, unlike the household of Caesar. In a Greco-Roman community or society, unity is maintained through unequal, hierarchical social relationships, which honor the elite or upper class and subordinate the lower class. In fact, equal membership in God's household is dangerous to the Roman Empire; Paul's radical message turns the whole ideological system of society based on unequal, hierarchical unity upside down. Stoics say society as a body is one; therefore, all members must conform to the cosmic unity of hierarchy. But Paul says that members of the Corinthian community should take care of each other because they are equal members of God's household. Indeed, it is God who chose the weak and the poor in the world (1 Cor 1:26–30). It is crucial to understand why Paul uses the human body as an analogy. He refutes a popular dominant metaphor of a social body in order to claim the body as an expression of holism and dynamism. As we see here, the issue for the Corinthian community is not a simple unity based in a body (like a social body), but a radical equality based in a solidarity in which all constitute parts of Christ (like a human body). "You are Christ's body, and individually parts of it" means "you have to live like Christ as you are attached to Christ's body (Christ's body as a way of life)." In sum, "you have to behave accordingly because you are united with Christ."

Christ's Body as His Sacrifice and Embodiment of God's Righteousness

Christ's body is interchangeable with Christ's faith when we read Rom 7:4 along with Rom 3:21–26 and Gal 2:16. "The body of Christ" appears in the former ("You have died to the law through the body of Christ") and "the faith of Christ" appears in the latter (Rom 3:22, 26 and Gal 2:17). Apparently, "the body of Christ" in Rom 7:4 is not an organism metaphor even with a cursory reading.[13] But it is Christ's body crucified, broken for others, as a result

---

13. Robert Jewett, *Romans: A Commentary* (Minneapolis: Fortress, 2007), 433–36. See also Kim, *A Theological Introduction to Paul's Letters*, 18–19.

of his embodiment of God's gospel. I have previously proposed the meaning of "dying to the law through the body of Christ" as follows:

> Declare a death to the law (the law of sin) that blocks God's principle of the law of love (God's law). "The body of Christ" in Rom 7:4 refers to Christ's own body (a subjective genitive)—the image of Christ crucified in particular. While God's law aiming at peace and life is not practiced in the world, Christ showed the way to it by challenging the power of the world and making solidarity with those who suffer from it. Christ's body represents his costly life because of his commitment to God's law (as God's love or righteousness).[14]

Likewise, we can interpret "the faith of Christ" *(pistis christou)* in Rom 3:22 and 26 as Christ's faithfulness through which God's righteousness (equivalent with God's gospel in Rom 1:1) has been manifested for all who have faith (Rom 3:22). It is Christ's faith that helps believers understand and experience the love of God (God's righteousness) through their "faith of Christ" (Rom 3:26). Here the faith of Christ is Christ's faith.[15]

Christ's Body as an Ethic of Christian Life

As a result of Christ's faith, shown through his obedience to the law of God (God's law of love, peace, and justice), believers are asked to imitate Christ's faith, which means "living of his body" (1 Cor 12:27: "You are *Christic* body"). Thus, Paul exhorts the Corinthians to imitate Christ (1 Cor 4:16 and 11:1).[16] Here, imitation of Christ is not a mere copy of his life but a participation in his life.

---

14. Kim, *A Theological Introduction to Paul's Letters*, 19.

15. Technical matters involve the translation or interpretation of the phrase "faith of Christ" *(pistis christou)*. Throughout this article, I read the Greek genitive phrases as subjective genitives, e.g., "the gospel of God" as God's gospel; "the body of Christ" as Christ's body; "faith of Christ" as Christ's faith. See further, Yung Suk Kim, *A Theological Introduction to Paul's Letters*, 2–5.

16. Kim, "Imitators" (*Mimetai*) in 1 Cor. 4:16 and 11:1: A New Reading of Threefold Embodiment," *Horizons in Biblical Theology* 33.2 (2011): 147–70.

What this means in Paul's logic is simple: "die and live." Carrying marks of Jesus, proclaiming Christ crucified to all people, believers participate in Christ's death and become a new creation (2 Cor 5:17). It is an ongoing journey of faith; believers experience the Spirit already, but the final victory of God is still coming. Until then, believers have to suffer and endure their salvation. So Paul says: "[I]t is no longer I who live, but it is Christ who lives in me. And the life I now live in the flesh I live by faith in the Son of God, who loved me and gave himself for me" (Gal 2:20).

In sum, the metaphor of Christ's body evokes the language of embodiment of God's love or God's gospel, for which Christ shows his faithful obedience to God's law (Rom 7:4); believers also need to imitate Christ (1 Cor 4:16; 11:1). The church (*ekklesia*) is the result of Christ's faith and the believer's participation at the same time. While the church is composed of various people, the lower class in particular (1 Cor 1:26–30), it also expands because of God's gospel (God's love), Christ's faith, and the believer's ongoing commitment to live for the gospel of God. Understood this way, "Paul's theology and ethics are informed by who God is, who Christ Jesus is, and who the believer (Paul) is."[17] This means that salvation is not done once and for all. Believers have to have Christ's faith. That is their participation in Christ's death or faith. Likewise, in Gal 2:16, believers are justified because of Christ's faith.[18] This means that believers can live righteously before God and people when they participate in Christ's faith or death. More surprisingly, we see in Gal 2:16 the Greek preposition *eis* ("into") before Christ, instead of *en* ("in"). "Believing into Christ" connotes the believer's participation in Christ's death. In fact, English translations hardly capture the subtle nuance of the Greek preposition *eis* that connotes the believer's action toward Jesus' death. Likewise, Christian identity

---

17. Ibid., 131.

18. If Paul wanted to convey the importance of the believer's faith in Christ (instead of Christ's faith), he could have used a prepositional phrase, like "faith in Christ" which we actually see in later epistles after Paul (Col 1:4,23; 2:5, 7; Eph 3:12; 1 Tim 1:13–16, 19; 2 Tim 3:15; 4:7). But Paul uses the Greek genitive form "the faith of Christ." See Kim, *A Theological Introduction to Paul's Letters*, 79—80.

is not fixed once and for all. Christian life is an ongoing faithful life modeled after Christ's life and death to embody God's gospel.

Recovering the Lost Tradition: Dynamic Aspects of Faith

I make a critical distinction between Paul's seven letters and the later epistles (Deutero-Pauline and Pastorals). I do not suggest that these later epistles are simply bad or useless because Paul did not write them. On the contrary, these later letters deal with legitimate issues for early Christian congregations (Eph 4:1–16). For example, if somebody in a congregation teaches that "Christ Jesus is not the right messiah or that your faith is nothing," then church leaders have to defend against those false teachers with the following advice: "Your salvation is secured in Christ." Subsequently, these leaders need to emphasize "what to believe" as a believer. What I describe here is one of the major issues that these later epistles address.

But if this particular aspect of faith overwrites the dynamic participatory aspects of faith that we see in Paul's theology and ministry, then I think it is a big mistake. To explain, let me use an analogy of a water dam of a power plant. The water contained in a dam is important for generating electricity. It has a potential to be transformed into electric power. To generate power, the potential water contained in a dam must fall from higher ground to lower. Otherwise, the water itself has no potential and is useless if it does not go through a managed process of power generation. In some cases, the water contained in a dam may be destructive if it is not controlled or managed by the secure locks. In the worst case, the water may turn into a flood, and sweep the whole city in seconds. This image of a dam may explain the diverse aspects of faith. Belief ("what to believe") is like the water contained in a dam; it is important for a person's faith and has potential to be effective in his or her Christian life, producing good works. But belief itself may be useless if it does not go through a process of a Christian life journey, which, I argue, involves the threefold embodiment of

God, Christ, and the believer. Put differently, Christians have to follow Christ by participating in his life and death for God's gospel that aims at all. In the worst case, the belief itself can be destructive to other people if not informed or processed by a sound theology and ethics (for example by the threefold embodiment). We see Paul's concerns about this kind of "blind" belief or knowledge at the Corinthian church. Some people claim they are "wise in Christ" without living the gospel of God as Christ did (1 Cor 4:10). Others boast about their knowledge, claiming that "all things are lawful" (1 Cor 6:12; 10:23). But Paul's advice is that "not all things are beneficial" (1 Cor 6:12; 10:23). Belief or knowledge should be checked and practiced wisely in the presence of others, aiming at God's gospel for all people in all circumstances.

In closing, I reiterate the centerpiece of Paul's theology of "the body of Christ." For Paul, "the body of Christ" has a double connotation in relation to the aspects of faith. First, Christ's body, understood as his broken, crucified, and humiliated body, shows his faithfulness in bringing God's gospel to the world. Christ's faith involves the true knowledge of God and the cost of embodiment for God's gospel. Second, Christ's body also has to do with a way of living for believers: "You are Christ's body" (1 Cor 12:27), which means "you are *Christic* body." Believers have to associate their lives with Christ's body, especially his broken, crucified body for God's gospel. Read this way, "the body of Christ" in Paul's letters, is not primarily about ecclesiology but about Christology that underscores Christ's sacrifice and faith to embody God's gospel. As discussed before, it is the later epistles (Deutero-Pauline and Pastoral letters) that emphasize secure Christian identity in Christ, and therefore that take "the body of Christ" to mean an ecclesiological body. This new reading of Paul's theology and ethics, based on Christ's faith and the believer's participation in Christ, challenges us today to rethink who we are as Christians. Can we still believe in the same God of both Jews and Gentiles? How should we treat others—as lost members of God's household, or as enemies of God? How can we participate in Christ's faithfulness for God' gospel? How can we maintain a connection between Paul's theology and ethics that balances the role between God, the Messiah, and ourselves? If Christ showed his faithful obedience to the love of God (God's righteousness), what should be our task other than living his life, his body, his faith, and his death so that we may also serve God's church?

Bibliography

Badiou, Alan. *Saint Paul: The Foundation of Universalism*, trans. Ray Brassier. Stanford, CA: Stanford University Press, 2003.

Barrett, C. K. *A Commentary on the First Epistle to the Corinthians*. New York: Harper & Row, 1968.

Bauer, Walter. Ed. *A Greek-English Lexicon of the New Testament and Other Early Christian Literature*, 3rd Edition. Chicago, IL: University of Chicago Press, 2001.

Benjamin, Walter. "On the Mimetic Faculty." In *Reflections: Essays, Aphorisms, Autobiographical Writings*, edited by Peter Demetz. New York: Harcourt Brace, 1987.

Betz, Hans and Margaret Mitchell. "1 Corinthians." *Anchor Bible Dictionary*, Vol.1. New York Doubleday, 1992. P.p 1139–48.

Black, Max. "Metaphor." *Proceedings of the Aristotelian Society* 55 (1954–55) 273–94.

Bornkamm, Günter. *Paul*, trans. D. M. G. Stalker. New York, NY: Harper & Row, 1971.

Bultmann, Rudolf. *The Theology of the New Testament*, Vol. 1. trans. Kendrick Grobel. New York, NY: Charles Scribner's Sons, 1951.

Castelli, Elizabeth. *Imitating Paul: A Discourse of Power*. Louisville, KY: Westminster John Knox, 1991.

Chadwick, Henry. "Origen, Celsus, and foe Resurrection of the Body." *Harvard Theological Review* 41 (1948) 83–102.

Copeland, M. Shawn. *Enfleshing Freedom: Body, Race, and Being*. Minneapolis, MN: Fortress, 2011.

De Boer, W. P. *The Imitation of Paul: An Exegetical Study*. Eugene, OR: Wipf and Stock, 2016.

Deissmann, Adolf. *Paul: A Study in Social and Religious History*, trans. William E. Wilson. London: Hodder and Stoughton, 1926.

Dodd, C. H. *The Epistle of Paul to the Romans*. New York, NY: R. Long & R. R. Smith, 1931.

Douglas, Mary. "Deciphering a Meal." *Daedalus* 101 (1972) 61–81.

BIBLIOGRAPHY

Elliott, Neil and Mark Reasoner, eds. *Documents and Images for the Study of Paul*. Minneapolis, MN: Fortress, 2011.

Farley, Wendy. *Gathering Those Driven Away: A Theology of Incarnation*. Louisville, KY: Westminster John Knox, 2011.

Gibbs, Raymond. *The Poetics of Mind: Figurative Thought, Language, and Understanding*. Cambridge: Cambridge University Press, 1994.

Gooder, Paula. *Body: Biblical Spirituality for the Whole Person*. Minneapolis, MN: Fortress, 2016.

Gudmundsdottir, Arnfridur. *Meeting God on the Cross: Christ, the Cross, and the Feminist Critique*. New York: Oxford University Press, 2011.

Henderson, Suzanne. "If Anyone Hungers, ...: An Integrated Reading of 1 Cor 11:17–34." *New Testament Studies* 48:195–208.

Holsten, C. "Die Christus-Vision des Paulus und die Genesis des paulinischen Evangeliums." *Zeitschrift für Wissenschaftliche Theologie* 4 (1861) 223–284.

Horden, Peregrine. "Pain in Hippocratic Medicine." In *Religion, Health and Suffering*, edited by John Hinnells and Roy Porter, 295–315. New York, NY: Routledge, 1998.

Ibita, Ma. Marilou. "A Conversation with the Story of the Lord's Supper in 1 Corinthians 11:17–34." In *1–2 Corinthians*, edited by Yung Suk Kim, 97–114. Minneapolis, MN: Fortress, 2013.

Jewett, Robert. *Romans: A Commentary*. Minneapolis, MN: Fortress, 2007.

Käsemann, Ernst. *Perspectives on Paul*, trans. Margaret Kohl. Philadelphia, PA: Fortress, 1971.

Keener, Craig. *The Mind of the Spirit: Paul's Approach to Transformed Thinking*. Grand Rapids, MI: Baker, 2016.

Kelly, Michael. "Mimesis." *Encyclopedia of Aesthetics*. New York: Oxford University Press, 1998. 3:233–46.

Kim, Yung Suk. *Christ's Body in Corinth: The Politics of a Metaphor*. Minneapolis, MN: Fortress, 2008.

———. *Messiah in Weakness: A Portrait of Jesus from the Perspective of the Dispossessed*. Eugene, OR: Cascade, 2016.

———. "Reclaiming Christ's Body: Embodiment of God's Gospel in Paul's Letters." *Interpretation* 67.1 (2013): 20–29.

———. *Resurrecting Jesus: The Renewal of New Testament Theology*. Eugene, OR: Cascade, 2016.

———. *A Theological Introduction to Paul's Letters: Exploring a Threefold Theology of Paul*. Eugene, OR: Cascade, 2011.

Kim, Yung Suk and Jin-ho Kim, eds. *Reading Minjung Theology in the Twenty-first Century: Selected Writings by Ahn Byung-mu and Modern, Critical Responses*. Eugene, OR: Pickwick, 2013.

Klauck, Hans-Josef. "Presence in the Lord's Supper: The Lord's Supper and the Lord's Supper Tradition: Reflections on 1 Corinthians 11:23b-25." In *One Loaf, One Cup: Ecumenical Studies of 1 Cor 11 and Other Eucharistic Texts*, edited by Ben F. Meyer, 57–74. Macon, GA: Mercer University Press, 1993.

Lakoff, George and Mark Johnson. *Metaphor We Live By.* Chicago, IL: University of Chicago Press, 1980.

Lee, Michelle V. *Paul, the Stoics, and the Body of Christ.* Cambridge, UK: Cambridge University Press, 2006.

MacMullen, Ramsay. *Roman Social Relations 50 B.C. to A.D. 284.* New Haven, CT: Yale University Press, 1974.

Marchal, Joseph. *Hierarchy, Unity, and Imitation: A Feminist Rhetorical Analysis of Power Dynamics in Paul's Letter to the Philippians.* Atlanta, GA: Society of Biblical Literature, 2006.

Martin, Dale. *The Corinthian Body.* New Haven, CT: Yale University Press, 1995.

Mercedes, Anna. *Power For: Feminism and Christ's Self-giving.* London: T&T Clark, 2011.

Mitchell, Margaret. *Paul and the Rhetoric of Reconciliation: An Exegetical Investigation of the Language and Composition of 1 Corinthians.* Louisville, KY: Westminster John Knox, 1992.

McGowan, Andrew. "The Myth of the Lord's Supper: Paul's Eucharistic Meal Terminology and Its Ancient Reception." *Catholic Biblical Quarterly* 77.3 (2015) 503–521.

Neugebauer, Fritz. "Das Paulinische 'in Christo.'" *New Testament Studies* 4 (1957–58) 124–38.

Odell-Scott, David. *Paul's Critique of Theocracy: A/Theocracy in Corinthians and Galatians.* New York: T&T Clark, 2003.

Patte, Daniel. *Paul's Faith and the Power of the Gospel: A Structural Introduction to Paul's Letters.* Minneapolis, MN: Fortress, 1983.

Polaski, Sandra. *Paul and the Discourse of Power.* Sheffield: Sheffield Academic, 1999.

Roetzel, Calvin. *Paul: Conversations in Context.* Louisville, KY: Westminster John Knox, 2015.

Schweitzer, Albert. *The Quest of the Historical Jesus: A Critical Study of Its Progress from Reimarus to Wrede,* trans. W. Montgomery. London: Adam and Charles Black, 1911.

———. *The Mysticism of Paul the Apostle,* trans. William Montgomery. Baltimore: John Hopkins University Press, 1998.

Smith, Dennis E. *From Symposium to Eucharist The Banquet in the Early Christian World* Minneapolis: Fortress, 2003.

Strauss, D. F. *Life of Jesus Critically Examined.* Cambridge: Cambridge University Press, 2010.

Taussig, Hal. *In the Beginning Was the Meal Social Experimentation & Early Christian Identity.* Minneapolis· Fortress, 2009.

Theissen, Gerd. *The Social Setting of Pauline Christianity: Essays on Corinth.* Philadelphia: Fortress, 1982.

Thiselton, Anthony. *First Epistle to the Corinthians.* Grand Rapids, MI: Eerdmans, 2013.

BIBLIOGRAPHY

Tripolitis, Antonia. *Religions of the Hellenistic-Roman Age.* Grand Rapids, MI: Eerdmans, 2002.

Welborn, Laurence. *Paul's Summons to Messianic Life.* New York, NY: Columbia University Press, 2015.

———. *Paul, the Fool of Christ: A Study of 1 Corinthians 1–4 in the Comic-philosophic Tradition.* London: T&T, 2005.

Wedderburn, A. J. M. "Some Observations on Paul's Use of the Phrase 'in Christ' and 'with Christ.'" *Journal for the Study of the New Testament* 25 (1985) 83–97.

www.ingramcontent.com/pod-product-compliance
Lightning Source LLC
LaVergne TN
LVHW051710080426
835511LV00017B/2839